*A Celebration
of Childhood
and Imagination*

the

# games

we

played

*Edited by*

Steven A. Cohen

*Simon & Schuster*

*New York   London*

*Toronto   Sydney   Singapore*

SIMON & SCHUSTER
Rockefeller Center
1230 Avenue of the Americas
New York, NY 10020
Compilation copyright © 2001 by Steven A. Cohen
All rights reserved, including the right of reproduction
in whole or in part in any form.
SIMON & SCHUSTER and colophon are registered trademarks
of Simon & Schuster, Inc.
Designed by Karolina Harris
Manufactured in the United States of America
10   9   8   7   6   5   4   3   2   1
Library of Congress Cataloging-in-Publication Data
The games we played : a celebration of childhood and imagination /
edited by Steven A. Cohen.
       p. cm.
     1. Games. 2. Toys. 3. Play. 4. Childhood.  I. Cohen, Steven A.
GN484.8 .G36 2001
305.23—dc21      Library of Congress Control Number: 2001020329
ISBN 0-7432-0166-3

A portion of the proceeds from this book will be donated to
S.C.O.P.E. (Summer Camp Opportunities Provide an Edge), a
program of the American Camping Association—New York Section. S.C.O.P.E. raises money to send underprivileged children to
not-for-profit summer camps.

The acknowledgments on page 173 constitute an extension of the
copyright page.

# *Acknowledgments*

The list of contributors to this book is long and luminous—too long to repeat here—but above all I'd like to thank the writers, journalists, actors, and other public figures who generously shared some of their most personal childhood memories. The skill and charm of their storytelling is one of the book's greatest delights. My deepest appreciation to all of them.

In addition, I'd like to thank Joe Regal, my agent, for his insightful counsel and unwavering support; without him this book would not exist. Thank you to Eric Schnure, who also gave me an incredible amount of his time and talent—Albom spent his

Tuesdays with Morrie; my Tuesdays with "Bubbe" were equally well spent.

Brad and Cori, your commitment to this idea and to our friendship are overwhelming. Brad, without you and, of course, John Chiarmonte, *TGWP* would never have taken off. For my friends Rusty and Elizabeth, Susan and Tim, and Porter, I am grateful for your early guidance, inspiration, and encouragement.

I am also thankful to my parents, my in-laws, and Jeffrey and Kim for being in my corner. This project was uncharted territory for me and your support helped guide me more than you know. Jay, thanks for all of the printing. Peggy Suntum, dinner was not nearly enough for all of your time and work. I'd also like to extend my gratitude to Andy Siegel, Jay Jacobs, and Jennifer Flax for bringing S.C.O.P.E. to my attention. And thank you to everyone who made a phone call or two or three . . . or lent their names to help put me in touch with a potential contributor.

When I first got started I had no idea what the job of an editor was. For me and this book, Constance Herndon was an advisor, supporter, cheerleader, and talented writer. Thank you for taking a chance on me.

Most important, my deepest gratitude to my bride, Eva. Your faith in me and your unconditional love carried me through this process. Thank you for believing me.

*For Eva, my love*

# Contents

# Contents

the
# games
we
played

# Introduction

When I was seven, a home run in a game we called Two Ball meant hitting the ball clear over the dog-house that sat at the far corner of the Alperts' yard. If you managed to avoid Mrs. Alpert's broom, that should have been worth two runs. When the Alperts and that mutt moved away and a German shepherd named Mozzie moved in, a fence replaced the doghouse and the game changed completely. Now it required two people just to retrieve the ball: one to play the position of Distracter, the other to actually stick his hand through the fence and grab the ball. Jason Glasser, the lanky kid down the block, was a Hall of Fame Distracter.

I don't remember the scores. I can't even tell you my batting average, although I certainly could at the time. But I can tell you that Mozzie had a red collar with a silver dog-bone nametag. That's because outfoxing Mozzie was as much fun as the game. Somedays, it *was* the game.

Willie Wonka said it best: "We are the dreamers of the dreams." And when we were kids, dreaming is what we did best. We invented games. Turbo Ball. Trip and Fall. Creek Walking. Roof Baseball. Sumo Soccer. Tennis Golf. Carpet Football. Swamp Man. Bunk Ball. Rules, boundaries, the number of players: we created them all. We had our own language and our own terms. We didn't care if it rained and we never got tired. The only limitations were our imaginations . . . and, of course, nightfall. But if someone had to go in for dinner, we just made up a new rule, and sometimes that generated a whole new game.

Growing up, I thought Mr. Alpert invented the phrase "Hey kid, get off my lawn!" It turns out that guy lives everywhere. It also turns out that the foul pole was just an oak tree, the end zone was where someone's yard began, the hockey rink was just Midfield Road.

In an age when computers, television, piano lessons, and soccer practice all compete for a child's attention, this book aims to recall a different time—a period when children's lives were less structured, less hurried, and less scheduled. When free time was actually free. In this book, that time is remembered by poets and playwrights, printmakers and a president, women and men from all across the country. Their stories may be different, but in each we recognize ourselves and are reminded of at least two things we all have in common—the gift of imagination and the wonder of childhood.

These are the games we played.

*Steven A. Cohen, age 8*

# The Game

## *Robert Pinsky*

No ball, no rules. Any one boy
On the cinder playground
Raises his hand and yells *I Got It*
And a few others chase him reaching
To touch him and the great
Game begins.

At first maybe four or five
Charge after him and one tags him
And yells *I Got It* and then more
Join the pack lunging after the new
Leader, the pursued one

Who sprints and dodges, head-feints
Nearly out of breath, writhing
Out of reach.

No end, no score.
Thrill of the broken field run in football, but
Pure: no boundaries, no goal.

No teams. Aristocratic martial
Rhythm of anarchy and brilliance,
The one against the many:

I remember a heavyset boy named Carl
Who liked to keep the chainlink
Fence to his back, even
Leaning against it, sidefaking and pulling
His chubby belly back, and every time a boy
Touched him, *I Got It,* Carl
Dancing tagged him back
With rope-a-dope hands *I Got It*
Back on the tagging arm, Carl
Unwinded at bay unyielding.

Sometimes the whole playground
Ran like one animal harrier
Streaming after you,

Challengers and thwarted in turn
Hounded and hounding, with grins
Like tired hounds.

And after the exhilarated spell
As the fox, the defiant
Scapegoat who dares all comers.

Always finally out of breath
You laugh and let yourself
Be touched, collapse thrilled
And exhausted to crouch panting
Hands on knees as you watch the herd
Speed on after the twisting shifting
Hero sooner or later always depleted
Of strength, unpetulant, capitulated
To the great ongoing
Entropy of the game.

ROBERT PINSKY was the United States Poet
Laureate from 1997 to 2000. He is the author of six
books of poetry, most recently *The Figured Wheel:
New and Collected Poems 1966–1996* (1996) and *Jersey*

*Rain* (2000). He teaches in the graduate writing program at Boston University and lives in Cambridge, Massachusetts.

# The Sweet
# Long Days

*David Maraniss*

On the afternoon of my tenth birthday in August
1959, my friends and I rode our bikes down to Vilas
Park in Madison, Wisconsin, to play with my favorite present. It was a new baseball, which came in
the mail after my parents sent in a coupon from Red
Dot Potato Chips along with a ten-dollar check. I remember how excited I was when I first rolled the
ball around in my hands and read the markings on
its shiny white cover. There, in cursive scrawl, were
the signatures of the great Milwaukee Braves: Aaron,

Matthews, Spahn, Burdette, Buhl, Covington, Bruton, Crandall. Three Hall of Famers graced that ball, yet the thought of stashing it away in a drawer for safekeeping or mounting it for display never seemed to cross my mind. Baseballs were for playing and this new ball was the only one we had, so we took it down to the park and used it to play Five Hundred.

Five Hundred was the least inventive of the many games we played, but one of our mainstays nonetheless, because it allowed us to chatter and tease and hang together yet still be ruthlessly competitive. While one guy hit grounders and flies, the rest of us congregated in a heckling mass out in the field, moving in or back depending on the hitter's power, scrapping and blocking and tripping one another to field the ball. You got 25 points for snagging a grounder, 50 points for a one-bouncer, 100 points for a fly, and minus the same amounts for an error. The first to 500 hit next. For anyone shuddering at the thought of mindless boys ruining a collector's treasure by pounding the prized signatures on the birthday baseball into unreadable smudges, it should be noted that the game that day ended swiftly, before any of us reached 500.

Winky saw to that. Winky was Madison's best-known resident, the elephant at the Vilas Park Zoo.

She lived by herself on the western edge of the old-fashioned zoo, whose small cages and limited spaces must have been an outrage to animal freedom fighters although they gave the place an accessible charm. Like the rest of the city, the Vilas Zoo had a free and unimposing air. It was situated right in the park, with no gates or fancy entrances separating it from the expanse of grass and ball diamond and picnic tables leading out along the Lake Wingra lagoon. All of the diamonds were occupied on that long-ago August afternoon, and Five Hundred did not require bases in any case, so we found our own playing field between a big elm tree and the elephant house. Without considering the consequences, we placed the batter down by the big elm with the high green bars of Winky's outdoor cage looming far behind the fielders like the outfield wall at Milwaukee County Stadium.

My friend Frank Roloff batted first and last. Frank was big and strong and nearly blind in one eye. His performance against live pitching was uneven, but when he got hold of the ball, it really flew. In my mind's eye, I can still see him tossing the ball in the air, whiffing, picking it up, tossing it again, whiffing again, picking it up, tossing—crack! Bobby Freed and Dave Roloff and Johnny Richards and I all look up as the birthday ball soars over our heads, bounces a few times, and rolls right through the wide green bars, coming to a stop near a bale of hay. And there stands Winky, her wrinkled gray trunk looping and swaying, looping and swaying, until finally she cradles the foreign object in a curlicue of rubbery trunk and picks it up and stuffs it into her mouth. She chews a few times and the ball comes hurtling out, landing on the cement so tattered and misshapen that it does not even bounce. Just splat! like soggy shredded wheat. And that is all there is of my prized present, and the guys are laughing, and finally I comprehend what has happened, and why, and how typically careless I have been, and though it hurts I smile along, until soon we all fall to the grass in a fit of mass hysterics, giggling and snorting about how Winky ate my baseball.

When that memory came back to me recently, my first impulse was to wonder where my parents were and why they didn't stop us from playing with the autographed ball. Then I realized that my parents were largely absent from my deepest memories of childhood not because I had blocked them out but because they simply were not there. The essential wonder of the games we played is that we played them blessedly free from adults. There were no soccer moms or Little

League dads. For better and worse, we defined and lived in our own world. Our landscape covered a square mile or two framed by the tunnels at Camp Randall Stadium on the east, the diving board at the Willows on Lake Mendota on the north, the reservoir near Hoyt Park on the west, and Vilas Park and Lake Wingra on the south. Within that territory we were native scouts who roamed free on our bikes (one speed, foot breaks, wobbly handlebars). We knew every shortcut, every grouchy old lady and loose dog to avoid, every patch of grass that could become a football field, every brick wall that could serve as a backstop for a game of broom ball, and every backboard where we could play H-O-R-S-E, the winner earning the right, in our fantasies, to kiss Ellen Dillinger or Sally Ylitalo.

I certainly have nothing against the parents of today who spend their weekends in minivans hauling gangs of uniformed kids from one organized sport to another, who slip out of work early on weekday afternoons to watch their daughters or sons compete. They are usually doing it as an expression of love, trying to show that despite their own busy lives they can find quality time for their children. Some might even be motivated by what they see as a deficiency in their own childhood, wanting not to repeat the cycle of an absent father who never watched a son's game. When my own son played baseball, I tried never to miss it, and one year I became so obsessed with showing him I cared that I attended virtually every practice. Yet I hold absolutely no grudge against my own parents. I know they loved me. It was just something about that time and place that allowed them and the other parents to stay away with no apparent psychological bruising on either side of the equation.

Childhood in Madison was for children. There was no Little League in our part of town, the near-west side. We played in the city league, which was overseen benignly by the recreation department. No adults were acting out fantasies of being major league managers or general managers, benching and trading adolescents. The umpires were high-school boys. My friends and I put together our own team, which usually left us short on pitching but long on camaraderie. We set the lineup, hit the fungoes, ran the infield practice, and passed out the schedules and jerseys.

Our uniforms were inexact, to be kind. Some of us wore spikes, some tennis shoes. Dan Siebens, our best athlete but already a bit of a bohemian, once showed up in sandals, which came flying off as he rounded first on a double. I don't know if any of us had heard of stirrups or sanitary socks. Our pants were jeans and khakis, all patched or with holes in the knees. But we all wore the same beloved jerseys.

And how *fine* those jerseys seemed. A few days before the start, the captains would pick up a pile of them at the rec office on West Washington, and that is when we would learn what our colors were, who our sponsor was, and how we would be identified for the rest of the summer. The jerseys were made of soft knit fabric, and they usually had collars and half-zippers. Once the jerseys arrived, our mothers had no need to wash shirts the rest of the summer. We wore them virtually every day, game or no. They were our gang colors, in a sense. You could tell friend or foe at a distance as swarms of red and black or green and white or maize and blue pumped and glided through the elm-shaded streets, gloves swinging from the handlebars of their bikes. The sponsors' names were on the backs, all local businesses from the neighborhoods: K&N Water Softeners, Findorff Lumber, Bowman All-Star Dairy, H&R Variety (We called it Hock and Run), Klitzner's, Klein-Dickert, Oscar Mayer, Octopus Car Wash, The Hub. In all the years we played, I don't think we ever met an adult from any of our sponsors unless they happened to be in the family. My dad, who loved baseball, rarely saw me play. I remember once when he came to a game at Vilas Park—the only way I knew he was there was because our third baseman, Mike O'Meara, caught a glimpse of a familiar profile, put up his glove to his face, and shouted at shortstop, "Hey, Dave, I think your dad's hiding behind that tree over there!" That image has stuck with me over the years and I recall it with wistful fondness, thinking back to the sweet long days when our parents let us live in our own world, and make our own mistakes, even if it meant that Winky ate my baseball.

DAVID MARANISS is an associate editor of *The Washington Post.* He is the author of *When Pride Still Mattered: A Life of Vince Lombardi,* and *First in His Class: The Biography of Bill Clinton.* He won the Pulitzer Prize for National Reporting in 1993 for his articles on the forces that shaped Bill Clinton's life. He lives in Washington, D.C., with his wife, Linda, who also grew up in Madison and remembers the jerseys.

# Paper Dolls

## *Esther Williams*

I grew up on the edges of a once-thriving truck farm community just southwest of Los Angeles, at 8722 Orchard Avenue, a rambling, single-story, wood frame house. My daddy practically built the house himself, at least enough of it to accommodate the five children my mother was to have. We had a backyard with pomegranate trees where we would hang the laundry to dry. The fruit came each year in the winter and we knew we would have pomegranate jam to last us throughout the year.

The family arrived in Los Angeles, in the teen years of the last century, to accompany my eldest

METRO-GOLDWYN-MAYER STAR

brother, Stanton, who had been signed to a "performing contract" in the burgeoning Hollywood movie industry. Stanton was a precocious seven-year-old who was small enough to play four. The money was just about enough to move the family from Salt Lake City, where my father had been a sign painter for the Wilkes Theater chain (originally we were from Dodge City, Kansas). Los Angeles was a step up from sign painting, although just a baby step since there was more promise than performance. Nonetheless Stanton costarred in several silent movies and toured in a theater production of *Eyes of Youth* with Marjorie Rambeau.

By the time I came along, money was scarce. I was actually born *in* the house because we couldn't afford the hospital. Despite Stanton's newfound stardom, Daddy found work difficult to locate, and when he did work he was rarely paid. Clothes and toys were hand-me-downs from brother to sister to brother to sister to me (and throw in a cousin or two). Since I was number five in the pecking order, nothing looked like the original. The stuffed toys were eyeless or earless, the pull toys minus at least one wheel. With three girls and two boys, toys had no sex. I was just as likely to play with my brother's broken slingshot as with my sister's raggedy doll.

When I was eight years old, tragedy struck the Williams family like a lightning bolt out of a Kansas sky. Stanton suffered a blocked colon and died on the back porch before we could even call for help. The grief that overcame my family remained with me for years. And the consequences were immediate, for Stanton brought in the most money. Daddy would never be able to match it. It was 1929 and the Depression hit us hard, as it did almost every other family in America. Daddy had had problems getting work before, but that was nothing like what we were about to experience. Every month we waited for the welfare box to bring us clothes and toys. One year we received a box that contained a doll with a porcelain head and for each succeeding holiday throughout the year, Daddy would paint a different face on the doll, change the color of its hair, and give it to me for my holiday gift.

My mother went to work, around this time, counseling other families on how to cope with their lot. My father, felled like a great tree, never seemed to get out of his easy chair, although "easy" seemed like a misnomer—I never thought there was anything easy around us.

Christmas was especially difficult. My aunt Clara and uncle Charlie usually brought us a tree from their farm outside of the city, and we all pitched in with decorations we had made throughout the year. Presents were functional. One year I saved enough spare change to buy my father a bar of Williams Shaving Soap. I was thrilled because it had his name on it—*Williams.* But on that Christmas, in 1931, my daddy really did something special for me. He may have done something equally nice for Maureen or June or David, I don't remember, but I knew he did something special for me.

In a little workshop he had in the back of the house, he had collected scraps of wood and bits of fabric, and without ever telling anybody what he was doing, he built me a dollhouse. Not just any doll-house, but a two-story dollhouse with pillars in front and a porch that went all around the house. He painted the house white with a red roof and green shutters. It looked just like a house I had seen in a book about the Pilgrims and George Washington. Inside he built bedrooms and stairs and a kitchen and a sewing room. And five little beds for the four bedrooms, and tables and chairs for the dining room. He built a couch and two chairs covered with remnants of a blue flowered chintz cotton that mother had thrown away after sewing herself a house dress, and a fireplace where the wood was painted red and yellow to look like a warm and welcoming hearth. And he made a wooden stool just big enough for me to sit on comfortably at eye level with my house. It was the most beautiful house I had ever seen. He sat me down in the corner of the laundry room, out of the way of the rest of the family, and said to me, "Well, Esther Jane, this is all yours, just for you. Now you fill it with the family you want." I threw my arms around about as much of him as I could reach and cried and hugged and told him "our family is the only family I *ever* wanted."

But I did create a family. I searched the magazines my mother would bring home from the counseling center where she was now employed and I'd cut out paper mothers and fathers, brothers and sisters, friends and strangers who would come and visit my house. My father taught me how to back my dolls with cardboard so they would stand sturdy. I would cut up the remains of the paper and design clothes for my new "family." I learned that if I left little paper tabs on each piece of the cutout clothing I would be able to dress my paper friends. They all had stories. I would reach deep into my imagination—although sometimes it didn't need to go much further than my last fight with my sister June, who yelled at me when I wore her favorite blouse to school and got an indelible ink spot on it. I tried to end everything happily but there were tragedies, of course, and I would have to tell my newly made friends, "Oh well, sometimes your dog dies and there is nothing you can do." We weren't religious but I had heard that you could always send whatever the problem was back to "God," whoever that was. I guess if I'd had a clear picture of "God" I would have made a paper cutout of him, too.

I was certainly occupied. From the breakfast table I went straight to my paper dolls before I left for school, and I returned to them to share the day when I came home. They were closer than friends. They were confidants—they were my secret world.

Little girls all over the world make up stories, make up families, compensate for the ones they don't have, make changes to the ones they do have, create scenarios in which events take imaginary turns and perhaps make life better than it is. Maybe our love of dolls is genetic, part of giving birth, part of nesting. Maybe it's just wishful thinking. As I grew older my fantasy, my dollhouse, my paper cutouts went one step farther.

When I walked on to my first set at MGM years later, in one of the Andy Hardy family series, to be exact, I knew at some subliminal level that I had been here before. The terminology was different. I was handed a *script,* put into *wardrobe,* told where to *meet my marks,* when to *cross,* by a *director* seated on a stool in front of a house that was no less real than the dollhouse my daddy set on the laundry room table.

The irony, of course, had not been lost on me. Years later the public relations department of MGM presented me with a promotional coloring book and paper doll cutouts of my own image, with clothes to match (and preset tabs). I knew the circle had come around in full.

Perhaps my father never realized how emblematic his dollhouse was for me. It wasn't necessary. He lived to see me reach the pinnacle of my career in the movies and he kept an Esther Williams scrapbook, which I treasure. As I looked back at photos of myself in newspapers and magazines, did I think that somewhere, some young girl was cutting me out to make a paper doll? Maybe I should ask Julia Roberts. . . .

ESTHER WILLIAMS, whose memoir *The Million Dollar Mermaid* was a recent bestseller, retired from the screen in the 1960s but has remained active through her involvement in both her own line of swimsuits and in the development of synchronized swimming as a competitive sport. She is married and lives in Beverly Hills.

# Ping-Pong Palace

## *Porter Shreve*

My father, whose name I share, was the Touchdown
Club's Schoolboy Athlete of the Year in 1957. As a
football tailback he made first team All-American; as
a basketball forward he was All-City four years
straight; in baseball the old New York Giants offered
him a contract to play shortstop; and in the spring
season, moonlighting for the track and field team, he
set school records in the long jump and high jump
and dominated every meet. If you go to the Malt
Shop near Wisconsin and Brandywine, a relic from
the days when Washington, D.C., was truly a small
town, you'll still find his picture up on the wall—

a six-foot-three golden boy with a reluctant expression standing beside Ted Williams and a waist-high trophy.

When I was a boy I made myself curator of the Porter Shreve Museum—a small collection that I maintained on the shelves of my bedroom closet. I had game pictures and newspaper clips, ticket stubs and letters from scouts, posed photographs of my dad dropping back for a pass or plowing into an imaginary line, the football tucked under his arm. I didn't tell my father about the museum. His career had ended abruptly on a routine running play in a preseason scrimmage his second year in college. His foot had gotten twisted among the bodies and broke in such a way that metal pins still hold it together. My closet was a private shrine to what might have been, so I kept the door closed.

I was not a bad athlete, but my mother's side of the family had brought flat feet, bad eyesight, and limited eye-hand coordination into the genetic mix. I would eventually be a role player—a cornerback assigned the opponent's second-best receiver; a point guard with a semireliable set shot; a singles hitter known for beating out grounders. Tossing the football and playing tennis with my father I was awed by his effortless athleticism. I must have realized that I could never hope to be so skilled and graceful.

Nevertheless, I did what a boy could do: For my eleventh birthday I asked for a Ping-Pong table. Since both of my parents were teachers my father wasn't wild for the expense, but my mother broke down and got it for me and we moved it into the dingy garage at the end of our backyard. I spent hours out there, playing game after game with my little brother and sisters, beating them 21–4, or skunking them 7–0. Even playing my youngest sister—she couldn't have been more than five—I'd scorch the white balls past her tiny head.

Eventually I was one of the best players in the neighborhood. Nobody could touch me on my home court. I was beating all of my friends and sometimes their older brothers, too. I stationed my siblings on either side of the net and called them ball boys, and every piece of change I could slip from my parents' dresser I invested in my Ping-Pong career. I had paddles designed for spin—topspin, backspin, sidespin, it was all in the wrist. For speed I went with sandpaper paddles, the kind that popped with a hollow sound, and against the better players, whom I had to finesse, I used a hybrid paddle, pimpled on the forehand side, sponge and rubber on the backhand.

My father showed little interest in Ping-Pong, occasionally coming out to hit the ball back and forth with us. He often played with his left hand, which charmed my siblings but irked me, and if I ever got too competitive he'd always make an excuse and go back inside. To personalize our clubhouse, I dragged my mother and my siblings up to the hardware store one day and bought several cans of orange and white paint. Within a couple of weeks we had covered the interior of the garage from beam to beam, right down to the table, in fresh coats of dreamsicle and christened it the Ping-Pong Palace.

Maybe because my father had thrived in organized sports, for the most part the kids in my family played conventional games. Sure, we raced sleeping bags down the stairs, built tent cities out of bedsheets, and invented personas for our Matchbox cars. Before the Ping-Pong table came into our lives we made as imaginative use of sticks and balls and fences and trees as any four kids. But during my two-year training to become Ping-Pong champion of the *whole* neighborhood, I put my imagination on hold.

My siblings and I set up an office in a tucked away room in the basement, an even grungier hole than the garage had been before we'd transformed it. In the executive offices of the Ping-Pong Palace, we hung *Sports Illustrated* photographs of Jimmy Connors and John McEnroe and other athletes of the late seventies, and we kept complicated statistics of our wins and losses versus each other and against kids in the neighborhood. We gave each paddle in the Ping-Pong Palace a name—Loopy, Spinner, Woody, Crusher, Hop Top, and Two Face—and then ranked ourselves and the paddles according to the hierarchy of an imperial court.

By the night of my thirteenth birthday party my reign as king was secure, but I nevertheless felt restless the way you do when you're growing out of something. My parents had invited most of my friends from the neighborhood, we'd had dinner and cake, and I'd just opened my last present—a five-ply basswood paddle with a two millimeter sponge covered in Flextra rubber—when my father asked, "Is there anything else you want for your birthday?"

I'd hauled in some fine loot to inaugurate my teenage years—a Walkman, a Stevie Wonder tape, the new paddle, and the latest version of Strat-O-Matic Baseball. So it seemed a strange question.

"How about some Ping-Pong?" I suggested.

"Since when did you have to ask?" he said.

"No, I mean I want to play *you*. Straight twenty-one. Best out of five. You against me, Dad, for the title of King of the Ping-Pong Palace."

A small cheer and some *ooooh*s went up from my assembled friends, and my father, after some gentle prodding from my mom, stood wearily to his feet and joined us all in the former garage.

I let him use the new paddle and chose for myself the reigning statistical champion—pimpled on one side, smooth on the other. We rallied for a while and I was pleased to see him playing with his strong hand. He was saying, "I haven't played Ping-Pong since the Army," or something to that effect, the way older men always do, but he didn't seem too rusty to me. His crosscourt backhands knicked the edges of the table, he kept the ball fast and low, and he served with a deceptive topspin that I often returned long. Our rally for serve alone must have been a couple of dozen shots before I finally won the point and he took me all the way to 18–21, barely losing the first game.

Game two was even tighter, 24–26. He made a great show at 20–21 of asking me exactly how the rules worked. "Oh, you've got to win by two? I had no idea. I thought you'd already won it," he said. But by game three he was loose and he beat me by four points.

Going into game four I grew nervous, short-handing my shots and getting frustrated. When he tipped a winner off the net at 11–9, I banged my paddle on the edge of the table. A clear mistake—he won going away 21–12.

In typical fashion, my father set down his paddle after the fourth game and said, "Hey, great. You're really a terrific player. Whaddya say we just call it a tie?"

Already I was over at the bench choosing a new paddle for game five. "But there's only one King of the Ping-Pong Palace." I took the statistics sheet from my brother.

"And the king is you," my dad replied.

I picked up the second-rated paddle—another hybrid combining speed and control—then returned to my end of the table.

"Come on. Just one more game," I pleaded.

He protested some more, as if his gifts were a burden, and then finally agreed.

Ping, pong, back and forth, we traded the lead a dozen times and wound up tied at twenty-one apiece. Then, for the next eighteen points, any time one of us had the advantage the other brought the score back to even, until, at last, with my father serving against my match point, I ripped a forehand deep off his serve and he returned the ball into the net.

Looking back I'm sure that my father scripted the

whole game. Shoeless Joe or Sly Stallone could not have done it better. I'd love to see a videotape: his half-lunging botched shots, his double faults to lose the serve, his unforced errors, which always seemed to occur after he had gained a match point. Just as pool sharks determine the narrative of their hustles, great players can see so many moves ahead that they are always in control.

My father must have known about the Porter Shreve Museum and he must have realized that it would do me a lot of good, with thirteen coming on, if he relinquished some of that hold. For him, it was as easy as missing a shot in a backyard game of Ping-Pong. No son of a golden boy All-American all-star could have asked for it much easier.

PORTER SHREVE is the author of a novel, *The Obituary Writer.* He is coeditor of three anthologies and his work has appeared in *The New York Times, Boston Globe, Salon,* and *Witness,* among other publications.

# On with
# the Show

## Glen Roven

Every block had one and I was it: the queer. I grew up in the early sixties in Flatbush, Brooklyn, long before queer had any sort of positive, ACT-UP connotation. It was merely one of the epithets hurled at me along with the usual fag, sissy, pansy, and homo—these were the words that supposedly wouldn't break my bones.

Naturally, I was excluded from all the block sports. I couldn't catch a ball to save my life and to this day I still throw like a girl. But, quite honestly,

I was *one thrilled outcast.* Being gay made me feel special, different from the Brooklyn thugs who lived on my block and the kids who would be stuck in Brooklyn for an eternity while I would make my fame and fortune in Manhattan. For an occasional nanosecond, I did miss the camaraderie of playing on a team. Although having a real friend instead of Lucille Ball and Wally Cleaver might have been nice, I had my world and they had theirs; I was fine with the uncrossable Rubicon between us.

For the other boys in the neighborhood the big game on Marlborough Road was stoopball. Most of the houses had two sets of steps leading up to the front doors. After buying a new Pensie Pinkie or a Spaldeen at Lamston's around the corner, the boys would spend hours throwing the ball against the upper set of stairs, each step having a higher point value, the lowest being five and the highest fifty. If you were able to throw the ball so that it didn't bounce on the way back to the street the points doubled. Occasionally, I was recruited to help with the math when my friends couldn't figure out what came after 1,999. I assured them it was a trillion.

Who wanted to play ball outside, anyway? I was quite content to stay in my room and play at something I seemed to have an innate talent for: big Broadway musicals.

These were not just any run-of-the-mill productions. These were *extravaganzas* complete with (homemade) costumes, an orchestra (my scratchy 78s on a little red portable record player), and a cast of thousands (the three girls on the block I could recruit)—each and every production directed by, choreographed by, and starring me.

The only cast albums around were my mother's old 78 recordings of Rodgers and Hammerstein shows. So my Broadway reviews consisted of the four of us lip-syncing to Mary Martin's "I'm Gonna Wash That Man Right Out of My Hair," or "Cockeyed Optimist" (although I was certain that the title was

"Cockeyed *Optometrist*" and consequently had the entire cast in cardboard cut-out glasses). We would usually end with the Grand Finale: "Oklahoma!" complete with a choreographed cow-roping section.

Where I picked this up is anybody's guess. I hadn't seen a Broadway musical yet, so it must have been the occasional movie musical on TV. Perhaps it was the perennial running of *Wizard of Oz* or *Peter Pan*. Maybe it's just in the genes. However this form of entertainment seeped into my consciousness, it filled my mind at a very, very early age. I'm sure my parents' friends never forgot my definitive version of "People Will Say We're in Love" sung to my sister's Chatty Cathy.

For those who are already shaking their heads in horror about the little gay boy putting on shows in his bedroom, I fear it gets worse. My parents took me to Balanchine's *Nutcracker* at the New York City Ballet, and my life changed.

Not that I became a ballet dancer, but I saw how magnificent professional theater could be. By a happy coincidence, the most celebrated, commercially successful Christmas show in NYC was also produced by the great titan of twentieth-century ballet. I venture to say any kid with artistic ambitions who had the momentous good fortune to see this production at an early age was forever changed. I still vividly remember the ballet's two children peeping through the keyhole trying to see the great Christmas tree. And then there was the theatrical coup as the painted scrim of the door dissolved through and we could see the guests actually trimming the tree. Amazing!

When I returned to my rehearsal room—bedroom—I knew I had to move on. Out were the tacky, under-rehearsed Broadway numbers with the amateurs from the block. Sorry Denise, sorry Suzie; I needed professionals. Luckily Elise Brodsky, a girl in my first-grade class, was already taking ballet lessons and when I first suggested a full-length production of the *Nutcracker* with a cast of two, she jeteéd at the chance.

Unfortunately, this production never came off and I learned a valuable lesson that would stand me in good stead over the years. Stars are different. Stars are temperamental. Stars *want* things. Elise and I easily divided up the solos in the ballet: She would be the Sugar Plum Fairy, I would be the Mouse King, she would be Marie, I would be Fritz. But when it came to the Candy Cane dance, we reached an impasse. She wanted it and I wanted it, too. In fact, I had already cut my hula-hoop in half so I could do the jumpy bit over the multistriped candy cane.

No matter what I did or how I pleaded, Elise wanted to dance that variation. I offered more money, better billing, the final curtain call, all the things that you learn to do early in the game. Still no movement. Negotiations collapsed. So I did what any budding entrepreneur had to do: I canceled the production. Artistic differences.

It was back to Broadway for me. Back to Mary Martin and the toilet paper wigs for "I'm Gonna Wash That Man Right Out of My Hair." Back to real show business. But when my parents bought me a sixties style tree lamp with three adjustable lights for studying, I knew I was right where I belonged. If I took a white sheet off my bed and painted a doorway on it, and if the tree lamp was positioned just right, we almost had a bleed-through effect. This wasn't a game. This was theater.

GLEN ROVEN, an Emmy Award winning composer, has his first musical, *The 5,000 Fingers of Dr. T,* opening on Broadway in the fall of 2001. He lives in London.

# Dominoes

## Gwen Ifill

Most of the games we played when I was growing up occurred indoors, mostly with people related to me by blood, around a kitchen or dining-room table. Now when I mention blood, I am talking about relatives and about sport. Although my family is very close, we played games as if our very lives depended on it.

Take dominoes. Many Americans are not familiar with this game and they are *surely* not familiar with the way West Indians play it.

My father was born in Panama; my mother and my three eldest siblings in Barbados. When they emigrated to the United States, they carried with them much more than just suitcases. They brought a belief in self-reliance and achievement as well as an instinctive knowledge of how to prepare rice and peas, fried plantains, and salt fish. And they brought the dominoes.

The dominoes were usually black wood with white dots on the face. As we prospered, my father invested in a sturdier, ivory-colored set with black dots. Whatever they were made of, they had to survive the abuse of West Indian dominoes players.

You see, it was never enough simply to place a domino on the table matching tiles as you went along. You had to SLAM it. You had to make the table shake, make the novices jump with the force of it, perhaps exclaim"HA!" to punctuate the brilliance of your play.

We call it trash-talking now. As on the basketball court, such loud, table-shaking play conveys a threat, intimidating your opponents into perhaps second-guessing themselves. . . . I know this sounds like we were flirting with violence at the same table where we broke bread. And maybe we were.

The way we played games in our family certainly doesn't fit the child-rearing standards of today, in which raised voices are supposed to threaten self-esteem. Psychological warfare as practiced at the card table was routine. But it taught me how to compete in a world in which the price of defeat is often intellectual humiliation.

It was also not lost on me that the loudest, most in-your-face players were the men and boys. Real dominoes playing requires a lot of testosterone. But more often I sought to mimic my mother, who could quietly slide a domino to the table and, BAM, wipe you out with one play, displaying only a quiet smirk. I learned a lot about making an impression without making noise by watching my mother play dominoes.

We didn't stop at dominoes, of course. Playing board games was an essential glue for us, especially during the holidays. Once the dishes were cleared and the leftovers put away, Monopoly reigned supreme.

Monopoly brought out the true character in each of us. My little brother, Ricky, was the fearless rogue. He would conspire with my father to build cartels. If he owned the orange properties and my father owned the greens, they would catch the rest of us going and coming, split the proceeds, and crush us with glee. God help us if Boardwalk fell into their hands.

My older brother, Bert, was the intellectual. He would snap up the railroads and use them as anchors to provide a steady income and a mortgage hedge. He also liked those purple properties. He'd snatch our Go money from our palms before we could fold it. I was hapless, grabbing whatever I could, winning only by sheer dumb luck, and tearing up pitifully when I lost. No one cared that I wept. It was a vital life lesson.

My friends now remark on how competitive my family seems. We have no idea what they are talking about. But we let them talk because that means they're distracted and we can WIPE THEM OUT.

As we grew older, we returned home for the holidays and inevitably pulled out the dominoes. We slammed them on the table and made fun of each other's boneheaded plays. And we sang. We sang hymns. We sang snatches of choral anthems. We sang West Indian jump-up songs and Harry Belafonte. We sang old standards. And just as the harmonies reached their satisfying conclusions, someone would punctuate the mood with a loud SLAM of the dominoes.

After all, winning was the point of the thing.

GWEN IFILL is moderator of *Washington Week in Review* and senior correspondent for the *Newshour* with Jim Lehrer, on PBS.

# Kid Crusher

## *Daniel Wallace*

My son is seven, and he wants a robot. He wants a robot that does anything he tells it to. This robot will bring him apple juice, find his socks, clean his room, and play with him whenever and wherever he wants to, all without complaining. In fact, the robot he has in mind will be thrilled to do it, absolutely thrilled. Though I know they've yet to invent anything like this—news I break to him gently—his description of the imaginary robot's ideal behavior is eerily familiar to me, and suddenly I realize he's not describing a robot at all.

He's describing my little sister.

My little sister, and perhaps all little sisters, functioned much the same as robots do. What makes a little sister particularly valuable to a boy is that, like a robot, she brings an uncritical approach to his ideas and suggestions, convinced that if the boy has had an idea at all, it must by definition be a good one. Other kids in my neighborhood had their own ideas, which were usually (according to them) better than mine. If I wanted to play hide-and-seek, they wanted to play kick-the-can. Sometimes I was able to persuade them that hide-and-seek was the quality suggestion ("I'm going to go home if we don't play hide-and-seek"), but by that time a lot of the *joie de vivre* had been drained from the activity, so I hid and sought without a child's twitter of delight.

My little sister, on the other hand, greeted everything I said and did with exultation, merriment, and total encouragement. I could fart for her—which, in fact, I'm sure I did—and she would find all aspects of it interesting and fun. As a baby, and without skills of her own, she was not much good to me. But as she grew and learned how to walk and talk and lift objects, she became an invaluable and treasured companion, a kind of indentured playmate.

The games we played were not really games, though I tried to make them seem like games to her.

That was the trick. For instance, I'd give her a challenge.

"How fast can you get me a cup of water? Can you beat your record? Start now, I'll time you . . . *go!* One one thousand two one thousand. . . ."

And off she went, as fast as she could move, out of my room, down the stairs, and into the kitchen, trying to beat her record of—what was it, fourteen seconds? I had no idea. When she brought the water back to where I was sitting, or lying down, watching television or talking on the telephone or simply reflecting on the enormous power I had over this seven-year-old girl, she'd ask me, "What was it? How fast this time?"

"You *almost* did it," I said, making up some number—fifteen seconds, sixteen—which was a good time, very good in fact, but alas, *not* the record. Still, better luck next time!

It did not stop at the water. Peanut butter and jelly sandwiches could be made and delivered under the same conditions.

At first I only wanted to be with her if I thought she could do something for me. But then, as time passed, a weird reversal took place and I found myself actually seeking out my sister as a playmate. I needed her. And it wasn't just because I got to do whatever I wanted to—which is a lie, of course. It *was* because of that, but not entirely. It was also because she was so wholeheartedly committed to whatever game I chose to do that we couldn't help but have a good time together. So even though it wasn't a relationship of equality, I think we both had an equally good time.

One of our favorite games was called Kid Crusher. This is the most primitive game I'm aware of: There are no sticks, no balls, no accessories of any kind. All it takes is two kids. One kid stands up on one end of a bed and a second lies down on the other end. The kid who's lying down begins to roll to the other side of the bed like a human steamroller, and the kid who's standing up jumps over him. This happens an infinite

number of times, or until the steamroller rolls over and crushes the kid. (Tip: The trick is to reverse direction as soon as the other kid jumps over you.)

Then there was the Sock Toss, another game of such prosaic simplicity it seems possibly Quaker in origin. At bath time, my sister's water would be run and she would get in, drawing the shower curtain behind her. Then I would enter the foggy room. In my hands would be a pair of socks which I'd taken off my own feet only minutes before. As the water ran I would throw them over the shower curtain, one at a time, and she would have to catch them before they hit the bath water. The degree of difficulty, of course, was titanic: I couldn't see her and she couldn't see me. Where was the sock coming from? Would it be a

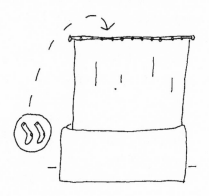

slow lob or a swift toss? Might it carom off the tiled wall? She either had to be very quick or commit in advance to a position: left, right, or middle of the tub. Heroic, diving attempts were sometimes made, the body splashing into the water so that it sloshed it out onto the floor, and all was silence. But then . . . ladies and gentlemen, *yes . . . a hand* would triumphantly peak out of one side of the curtain, holding in it the mostly white, mostly dry, sock. In the end, of course, she would fail, the socks would hit the water, and another element of the game began. It was called the Wet Sock Toss.

I don't remember how long these games went on. One day she caught on to the whole I'll-time-you thing and never did another favor for me for the rest of my life. The Sock Toss died next, because eventually it began to appear unseemly, to be in the bathroom with your brother, even with the curtain drawn.

But Kid Crusher lasted. It had all the aspects of the perfect game: playfully competitive, suggestively dangerous, and the playing field was really soft. Eventually we abandoned the bed for the neighbor's trampoline, but one day, trying to avoid being crushed, my sister jumped completely off it and when she hit the hard cold ground her left ankle broke. And that may have been the last time we played Kid Crusher together, ever.

Kid Crusher lives, however. I play it with my son now. He's a novice, and he has yet to figure out the speed with which I can change directions, rolling one way until he commits to his jump and then, while he's still in midair, moving in the other, trapping his feet and then his entire body beneath my rolling body, so that the two of us are spinning across the bed in a kind of mobile hug, laughing. It's hard to say what's happening here, as I'm playing this game with him. There's a father and a son, a brother and a sister, the past, present, and future all coming together within me like a sandwich made out of hope and memory, and suddenly I realize: It's like a tradition. Kid Crusher is a family tradition, something I'm passing on to my son, who will pass it on to his kid and so on, forever and ever, amen. And yes, it's kind of gratifying to imagine my grown son trying to convince his own kid to stop playing with the damn robot.

Get on the bed, he'll tell him. I've got a *real* game to show you.

DANIEL WALLACE is author of two novels, *Big Fish: A Novel of Mythic Proportions* and *Ray in Reverse.* He lives with his son in Chapel Hill, North Carolina.

# My Childhood: Skips and Stoops, Sisters and Saturdays

*Al Roker*

I wasn't a great athlete growing up. I never threw the winning touchdown pass and I never cleared the bases with the game on the line. I did have a decent garbage hook shot, but I was counted on more to clog up the middle and break up the other team's momentum. I guess everyone has a role. Growing up in Queens, mine was definitely not that of all-star.

But that was fine. For me it was never really about the game. I was just happy to be out there. Maybe that's why my memories aren't of *the* winning moment, they are of the wonderful moments in between.

I remember my mother sending me out to play in a pair of Skips. Skips were a no-name pair of sneakers that were sold at stores such as Sears. Wearing those on the playgrounds was the ultimate in uncool.

I would show up wearing my Oxfords; anything to avoid being caught in a pair of Skips. At least in my Oxfords I could say my mother accidentally threw out my sneakers, or something, anything. I could also blame the shoes on missed shots or bad plays. But I begged and whined and wheedled until finally my Skips were magically replaced by a pair of Converse: Now there were no more excuses.

But I recall a fate worse than Skips—having to take my sisters along to play. I'm the oldest of six, three boys, three girls. The girls—well, they were girls, and they ruined everything. I can still hear my mom calling out as I'd break for the door: "Al, take your sisters with you."

I'd mumble, "Ah, geez, Mom. Do I hafta?"

Mom would answer in that famous maternal tone.

You know the one—half inquisitive and half-irritated. "What's that, Al?"

"Nothing."

Life had a certain simplicity. Our parents didn't have to keep an eye on us because odds were there was always a parent in the community within eyeshot or at least earshot. We knew that if they saw us, the Parent Network would go into effect. Chances were, by the time I got home my parents would be lying in wait for me. They knew what I did; they had it chapter and verse. I couldn't even lie about it because they had the facts: "At 10:19 A.M. you were seen scaling the fence. . . ." "All right, I did it, I did it. You got me. I confess." I hated the Parent Network.

We lived in this little part of Queens. To me, that's what New York City really was—a collection of little neighborhoods. It still is. Today, people think New York City is what they see on TV. But Queens or Brooklyn, Staten Island or the Bronx— they're just like anyplace else. We just had different accents.

Everything started on the stoop. Not on our stoop. A good stoop had to have the right "feel." It maximized the number of guys who could fit into a small area through combined vertical and horizontal seating. Ours had my mother's fairly extensive plant-ings; it wasn't a place for what she called "young ruf-fians." So we'd usually go next door to the Segrees' house and hang out on their stoop.

We spent more time deciding what "to do" than actually "doing."

It always went the same way:

"What do you want to play today?"

"I dunnno. What do you want to play?"

"Wanna go up to the park?"

"I dunno."

We would blow up to an hour just trying to figure out whether we were going to play in the street or go up to the park. That was before the long debate even started on what we were actually going to play. Most times we would get tired of talking about it and somebody would finally say, "Let's just . . ." and everybody else would say, "Fine."

But we only had to make it through the morning, because Saturdays were special: The afternoons were reserved for dads. That's when fathers and sons would mix it up. When we were kids, it was fun to have your father playing punch ball or touch football for an entire afternoon.

My dad was a good athlete. In fact, we used to pile into the family station wagon and drive to Brooklyn to watch him play softball. But what I always admired about my father was that even though he was very athletic and his son wasn't, he never pressured me.

My dad and I watched sports together. The first time I ever saw a game live was when my dad, my uncle Champ, my cousin, and I took the subway to Yankee Stadium. I had watched many games on television and Yankee Stadium looked big, even on my small black and white television set. But that was nothing like being there.

I'll never forget coming out of the dark tunnel into the brilliant sunshine—it was amazing. But what I really remember is being most interested in what we were going to eat.

Uncle Champ asked me, "Did you come here to eat or to watch baseball?" and I thought, "Is this a trick question?"

But most of all, I remember that I loved being a kid. Everything about it. Yeah, even the Skips and my sisters. But do me a favor—don't tell my sisters that.

AL ROKER is the weatherman and feature reporter of NBC's *Today Show* and the author of *Don't Make Me Stop This Car! Adventures in Fatherhood.*

# The Cape

## *Judd Winick*

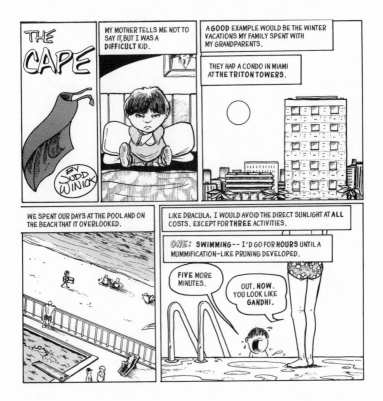

THE CAPE

BY JUDD WINICK

MY MOTHER TELLS ME NOT TO SAY IT, BUT I WAS A **DIFFICULT** KID.

A **GOOD** EXAMPLE WOULD BE THE WINTER VACATIONS MY FAMILY SPENT WITH MY GRANDPARENTS.

THEY HAD A CONDO IN MIAMI AT **THE TRITON TOWERS.**

WE SPENT OUR DAYS AT THE POOL AND ON THE BEACH THAT IT OVERLOOKED.

LIKE DRACULA, I WOULD AVOID THE DIRECT SUNLIGHT AT **ALL** COSTS. EXCEPT FOR **THREE** ACTIVITIES.

*ONE:* **SWIMMING** -- I'D GO FOR **HOURS** UNTIL A MUMMIFICATION-LIKE PRUNING DEVELOPED.

**FIVE MORE MINUTES.**

OUT. **NOW.** YOU LOOK LIKE **GANDHI.**

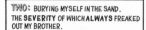

TWO: BURYING MYSELF IN THE SAND. THE **SEVERITY** OF WHICH **ALWAYS** FREAKED OUT MY BROTHER.

IT'S IN HIS **HAIR**!

AND THREE: SITTING IN THE CABANA DRAWING.

WHAT **ALWAYS** BROUGHT ME OUT OF THE DARK, THE SAND OR THE WATER...

WAS THE CAPE.

I HAD A RED **SUPERMAN** CAPE. GIVEN THE OPPORTUNITY I WOULD WEAR IT **ALL** DAY.

BUT FOR THE SAKE OF SANITY, PHYSICAL EXHAUSTION, **AND** THE QUESTIONABLE DURABILITY OF THE SWATH OF NYLON FABRIC MY DAD HAD SET A SCHEDULE.

IS IT TIME?

NOT YET.

NO CAPE UNTIL A **QUARTER** TO THREE.

AND WHEN A QUARTER OF THREE CAME, I'D HAVE THE CAPE TIED AROUND MY NECK--

AND I WENT **MAD**!

I'D "*LAUNCH*" HARD OFF THE GROUND, EMULATING **GEORGE REEVES** FROM THE FIFTIES *SUPERMAN* TELEVISION SERIES, I SUPPOSE...

POOT

AND I'D FLY.

AND FLY.

AND FLY.

AND FLY.

I'D GO FOR HOURS.

WE ALL DID STUFF LIKE THIS AS KIDS.

WHY?

73

WELL, WHY DO DOGS SHOVE THEIR HEADS OUT OF MOVING CARS?

Y'EVER DO IT?

IF YOU *HAD*, YOU'D *NEVER* ASK "*WHY*."

IT MADE A CRABBY KID-- **EUPHORIC.**

FWEP FW FWEP FWEP FWEP

JUDD WINICK is the author of the graphic novel *Pedro and Me,* creator of the comic *The Adventures of Barry Ween, Boy Genius,* and the writer of DC Comics' *Green Lantern.*

# Like It Was Yesterday

## Bill Clinton

Growing up in the South was hot so we were outside
all the time. You could be outside twelve months a
year; it was sometimes seventy degrees on Christmas
Day. There was the sense that we just lived outside.
And if we were outside, we would make up a game. . . .

From age eight until I was fourteen, I was playing
games constantly. All the obvious ones: touch football, softball, and hide and seek. Hide and seek was
fun because we lived in a great place with a lot of
bizarre nooks and crannies.

When we didn't have enough people to put together a game of football or softball, we would just make up a game. We used to play one particular game over and over again. All it required was a ball and a bat and at least two players. Either you could pitch to the batter or the batter could just throw the ball up and hit it. The fielder, of course, would try to catch it. If he could catch it in the air, then he got to bat. But, if he didn't catch it in the air—which was most of the time because we would try to hit it on the ground—then he had to field the ball and stop right where it was fielded. The batter would then put his bat on the ground and the fielder would roll the ball at the bat. If he hit the bat, then he became the batter. But if the ball bounced up and the batter was able to catch it, he got to keep batting.

The key was to field the ball quickly—the quicker you could get to the ground ball, the shorter the distance you would have to roll the ball. But you also had to learn how to roll the ball essentially *on* the ground; you didn't want it to bounce very much because it could bounce over the bat. It actually had to hit the bat. It was very good training for fielding and for directional control—rolling the ball made it almost like a bowling game.

I used to play a lot with my friend David Leopoulos, who lived only about two blocks from me in Hot Springs. Sometimes we would play with another friend of ours who lived a few more blocks away. And once in a great while we'd have as many as four. But usually it was two or three. My brother, Roger, was ten years younger than me, so he wasn't old enough to play with us.

We normally played in the back of my house. There was a drive up a hill, and then it was gravel, and then I had a little grass yard to the right as you faced the house. So you might catch the ball on the grass, you might catch the ball on the gravel, but either way, part of the rolling of the ball had to take place over the gravel.

I should confess—David and I used to play one not so nice game. We had two huge oak trees in my front yard, one of which had a lot of hedges around it—it was perfect for hiding. David and I would gather acorns and hide behind the trees. Right in front of my house was a thoroughfare, Park Avenue. We would wait for the cars to go by and try and hit the hubcaps with our acorns. We never tried to hit the cars—anybody could hit a car going by. The idea was to hit the hubcap, because it made the loudest, most delicious sound. Although sometimes if a pickup went by, we'd try to land the acorn in the back of the pickup. But we never wanted to hit a windshield or do any damage.

But one time we hit a guy's hubcap and it sounded like the world was coming to an end—BONG! The guy put on his brakes, stopped the car, and pulled over. He came racing up in our yard and we ran and ran. Thank goodness nobody was home to beef to.

Both my folks worked. My mother usually got home by the middle of the afternoon, because she started at 7:00 A.M. Very often she was there when I got home from school or shortly thereafter. But the neighborhood was like one big family. Right across the street in the back of my house there was a family that I was very close to. They had three children and they're all still friends of mine to this day. I spent tons of time in their house.

We also used to go to an old-fashioned little grocery store that was part of a mini–shopping area from the fifties. Nearby was a washeteria where you would wash your clothes. We used to go there and get soda pop all the time. There was also a great barbecue place called Stubby's Barbeque. We would sometimes go there—even when we were kids—just to get a sandwich and baked beans. Stubby's had these old-fashioned wooden tables and benches, including one table that was right in the front of the window, and we would sit there for hours and watch the traffic go by. I remember that like it was yesterday. We thought we were very important.

To me, childhood was about friends and discovery. When I think back on it, I think about how wonderful it was to be outside, even if I was getting stung by a bumblebee or dodging a rattlesnake, or handling tarantulas or centipedes or scorpions—and we had lots of them. Sometimes we'd even cut up the centipedes and watch the sections crawl on each other—our own little laboratory experiment. Everything we did became a game. That's the way it ought to be.


BILL CLINTON was the forty-second president of the United States.

# Bottle Cap Soldiers

## David Baldacci

It wasn't that I didn't have a goodly number of toys growing up, because I had my share. As a youngster, my interests tended toward the typical boyish pursuits, namely fighting, running, falling, throwing. However, my daydreams were where the real action was.

While others in my class did their multiplication tables, I was the battle-scarred leader of a small but dedicated squad of similarly situated young, vibrant men carved from rippling muscle, hair free of cowlick, who were often called upon to defend my cherished elementary school against attack from invaders of truly wicked pedigree. During these frothing, cataclysmic struggles I would, with inches to spare, snare the assistant principal from certain death, even though only the week before he had given me an unreasonable detention. I would rescue all the teachers from a fate worse than having to sing in the school choir. Lastly, in my arms would fall a certain upper-grade schoolgirl who had claimed my heart for that week. Sometimes I would lie dying, my lion's heart near beating its last, my pure blood spreading on hallowed, hard-fought ground. The magnitude of it routinely moved me to my own tears. I remember once an anxious schoolmate, seeing the drops of water falling on my work paper, leaned over and whispered, "Don't worry, it's not that hard: eight times eight is sixty-four."

The only experience that comes close to my vivid daydreams was the truly splendid, all-encompassing, titanic world wars I routinely orchestrated using the sacrosanct—veterans use the phrase only in a hushed voice—*Bottle Cap Soldiers.*

At my request, my father would bring home sacks of used bottle caps from his office soda machine. I did not care much for Coke or Pepsi or 7-Up. As any true aficionado of bottle cap wars knows, the *crème de la crème* were Nehi grape and orange, with an occasional lemon-lime thrown in, perhaps to be used as spies working behind the lines or as members of the Red Cross. Over the years I assembled armies of bottle cap soldiers by the thousands. My room, the garage, the backyard, the attic, and, to my parents' nightly horror as skin touched cold metal, their bed—the whole house would burn with the ethereal blend of orange and purple going at it without regard to international laws of conflict. They were simply out to win. And above it all I would lurk, managing the skirmishes and planning alternate strategies for my ridged metal warriors who had begun life as mere holder-backers of carbonation. It would be up to me to decide, in Godlike fashion, who would live, who would die—the dead were flipped over, their brilliant colors replaced by dull gray—and who would be COWs, a technical term meaning "caps of war."

My father tolerated these goings-on with relative calm and understanding, principally motivated, I realize, by the fact that the bottle caps were free. This, of course, allowed him to spend his money on other worthy pursuits such as professional therapy for my long-suffering brother and sister, who often fell victim to the complicated plots of their younger sibling.

It's tough to find Nehi bottle caps these days, and my armies have long since vanished. However, playing with my own children, I can sometimes hear the old battle cry of the caps. I can visualize the impossibly long lines of purple and orange heading inexorably toward their world-shattering collision. And sometimes I even conjure up the image of the fetching sixth-grader and the mini-skirted substitute teacher each resting comfortably on one of my arms, as their forever hero goes forth to battle once more.

DAVID BALDACCI is a critically acclaimed international best-selling author of numerous novels, screenplays, short stories, and essays. He lives in his native Virginia.

# Cow-Man

## Tony Earley

During the winter, Robbie Frazier and I played basketball for two or three hours every day after school in the driveway behind his house. We played until our fingertips cracked open along the whorls of our fingerprints, until our heads steamed in the cold; we played until the basketball contracted to the size of a cantaloupe and bounced as if it were made out of glass. Every time a car passed Robbie's house, we imagined that Carolina coach Dean Smith was driving it and that he would slam on the brakes, get out, and tell us that the Tar Heels could use a couple of players as good as we were. We imagined this over and over, for years.

Once or twice a year Robbie was visited by his

cousin Little Louis. Little Louis didn't care for basketball but he was very, very smart. When Little Louis was six or so, he challenged me to a game of chess in front of Robbie's whole family. Fifteen minutes later he said, "Check mate, you fool."

"You mustn't call other people names," Little Louis's mother said.

"Apologize to Tony," said Big Louis.

"I'm sorry," Little Louis said. "But I can't believe you fell for that. A *fool* could see that coming."

One afternoon when Robbie and I were playing basketball for the one-on-one championship of the world, Little Louis's mother made him come outside to watch. He was wearing a big coat and a ski cap. He looked like a miniature polar explorer. I took a jump shot and missed badly. The ball went out of bounds.

"That was terrible," said Little Louis.

"I know," I said as I went after the ball.

"I mean, it didn't even hit the rim," said Little Louis.

"I know," I said, and tossed the ball to Robbie, who took it out of bounds.

"It was an *air ball,* for gosh sakes," said Little Louis. "What's the point of practicing as much as you do if you still shoot like that?"

"Check," I said. Robbie tossed me the ball. I turned on Little Louis. I said, "Little Louis, if you don't go back inside right now, Cow-Man is going to eat you."

Little Louis blinked. "What's Cow-Man?"

"Cow-Man's got a body like the Incredible Hulk, but a head like a cow," Robbie said. "He lives in the woods."

I pointed at the trees across the field behind Robbie's house. "Those woods," I said.

Little Louis glanced at the woods and then he looked me in the eye. "There's no such thing as Cow-Man," he said.

"Suit yourself," I said.

Little Louis looked at Robbie.

"We saw him yesterday," Robbie said.

"I don't believe you," said Little Louis.

I shrugged. "It's your funeral."

"Why does Cow-Man live in the *woods?*" Little Louis asked shrewdly, searching for a flaw in our story.

"Where would you live if you had a head like a cow?" Robbie asked.

"Why doesn't he eat *you,* if he's so mean?"

"He likes to watch us play basketball," I said.

Robbie hoisted one from out of bounds and drained it. "He's a Carolina fan," he said.

"That doesn't count," I said. "You were out of bounds."

"Why does he like to watch you play basketball?" Little Louis asked. "It's so boring."

"Cow-Man's very lonely," I said. "He was going to

go to Carolina on a basketball scholarship but then he grew a head like a cow."

"That made him so mad he ate a bunch of people," Robbie said, going after the ball. "That's why he has to stay in the woods."

"But he still likes basketball," I said. "We're safe only as long as we keep playing."

Robbie bounced the ball twice and looked nervously across the field.

Little Louis stared at the woods a long time, then put his hands on his hips. "I still don't believe you," he pronounced. "I don't believe you at all."

"Rob?" I said. "Did you hear that?"

"Hear what?" asked Little Louis.

"Moo," said Robbie.

Little Louis jumped. "Stop that," he said.

"There it is again," I said. "It's getting closer."

"Moo," said Robbie, holding his index fingers up beside his head like horns.

Little Louis backed a step toward the house. "I said quit it," he said.

"I've never heard him that close before," I said. "Quick, bounce the ball, Robbie."

"Moo," said Robbie, pawing the ground with his foot.

Little Louis ran up the stairs and into the house. After a minute, the door opened and he stuck his head out. "My mother said there's no such thing as Cow-Man," he yelled.

A little later Big Louis came outside and stood beside the court. We could tell someone had sent him. "You really scared Little Louis," he said.

"We're sorry," I said.

Big Louis looked like he wanted to laugh. "You say Cow-Man's got a body like a man but a head like a cow?"

I nodded.

"And he lives in those woods and eats little boys?"

I nodded again.

"I'm going back inside," said Big Louis. "It's not safe out here."

"Moo," said Robbie.

When I was walking home that night, the woods seemed a lot closer than usual. I thought I heard something, an angry snort maybe, the clack of a horn against a sapling. I bounced the ball loudly. That night I ran home.

TONY EARLEY is the author of the short story collection *Here We Are in Paradise,* the novel *Jim the Boy,* and a collection of personal essays *Somehow Form a Family.* A native of western North Carolina, he lives with his wife in Nashville, Tennessee, where he teaches creative writing at Vanderbilt University.

# Lollipops
# and Lies

## *Susan Richards Shreve*

Fifth grade: Not old enough for freedom or young enough for children's games, outsiders by temperament, Tommy and I hung out on my front porch overlooking the playground across the street. Drinking lemonade from my parents' wine glasses, we watched the regular kids—the athletes on the blacktop and the club girls by the water fountain and the teenagers with their cigarettes and cherry cokes slouched by the swings. Sometime during the fall of that year while we were making plans to take over the neighborhood the Lollipop Garden was born.

The plan was simple. In a casual kind of a way, not to alarm the younger children in the neighborhood, but simply to engage their interest, we let it be known that on a Saturday the week before Halloween, we'd be creating a lollipop garden on the dirt patch underneath the Watsons' back porch. The Watsons were very old and we figured they wouldn't notice if the Symbionese Liberation Army moved into their kitchen.

The news got around and things being what they were back then in the Cleveland Park section of Washington, D.C., children under the age of eight were allowed to travel alone a block or two away from their own home without protection. The first Saturday, ten children ranging from five to nine crawled under the Watsons' porch with us.

I had stolen seeds from my mother's little gardening shed, choosing zucchini or eggplant or yellow squash, one of the vegetables I used to slide in my napkin at dinner and slip into the trash.

We allowed the children five seeds each. On their knees, their solemn faces reflecting the seriousness of the task, they put the tiny seeds in the damp, musty swamp that is the earth of the city of Washington.

"Next Saturday," we told them. "Come at the same time and the seeds will have grown into lollipops."

The following Friday, Tommy stopped by the 5&10 on his way home from detention and stole a bag of lollipops. He was quite professional at thieving.

The next day Tommy and I met shortly before the appointed time and stuck the lollipops in the ground in neat rows.

This morning there were twice as many children arriving at the Watsons' porch, all in a state of wild excitement. In only a week the lollipops had grown full size complete with sticks and cellophane wrappers. We allowed the children to pick the ones they had planted.

By the next Saturday, the news had spread and a regular army of children arrived almost before we had finished our lollipop planting.

"Are you magic?" one of the younger horticulturists asked, full of unbridled enthusiasm and admiration.

"Not only are we magic," Tommy said in a whispery voice he put on for the benefit of small children, "but *you* are magic too."

And so it went, our perfect little kingdom, until the week before Thanksgiving. That Friday, Tommy reported to me later, he was a little distracted by the comic book section of the drug store. The lollipops he had taken in the candy section and stuck under his jacket were hanging out from underneath the coat and the clerk stacking the shelves with magazines had noticed.

"What do you have there?" she asked.

"Nothing," Tommy replied.

"It doesn't look like nothing to me." So she called the manager, who took Tommy to his office and notified the police. Tommy called me and asked was I willing to admit to being an accomplice. To which the answer was yes.

So the police came and Tommy's father came and by dinnertime the lot of us, including my parents and me, were sitting in the Eighth Precinct talking about shoplifting. These were the late fifties when criminal activity among children was perhaps less frequent. In any case we were a big deal.

"So," the policeman said to Tommy and me. "Tomorrow when the children in the neighborhood come to this Lollipop Garden you've lied to them about, you will be there and so will I." He had his arms folded across his chest, very pleased with himself, as I remember. "You will tell the children exactly what happened—how you stole the seeds and stole the lollipops and pretended to be magic when you were simply thieves."

"I'd prefer a juvenile detention home for a few months," Tommy suggested.

The following morning we waited beside the Watsons' porch. Some distance away, the policeman leaned against a tree.

"I feel sick," I said to Tommy as we watched the children hurrying in twos and threes down the block toward us. Tommy's face was the color of milk.

"What're you going to say?" I asked him as the children rushed up to us, ducking under the porch. He shook his head.

"Nothing grew," the first child said.

"Maybe it's too cold?" another asked.

"What happened to our poor seeds?" A little boy was beginning to weep.

"They didn't grow this week," Tommy said quietly.

"Because it's cold?" the boy asked.

"Because there wasn't any sun?"

"Because of what?" the little boy asked.

"Because I got caught stealing the lollipops from the 5&10," Tommy said. "And so we didn't get to stick them in the ground this morning."

"I'm sorry," I said. "We're both really sorry."

But the children weren't listening. Slowly, their heads down, their bodies folding like so many paper bags with a sadness beyond measure, they walked away from the Watsons' porch onto the mossy brick sidewalk, and home.

SUSAN RICHARDS SHREVE is the author of twelve novels, most recently *Plum & Jaggers.* She is also the author of many books for children and has edited four anthologies. She teaches in the Masters of Fine Arts Program at George Mason University.

# The Basement

## *Alan Shapiro*

How many years, decades since I'd even thought of
  Gary
when my mother told me on the phone the other
  night,
in passing, that he'd been thrown in jail for kiting
  checks,
and that this on top of all the other heartache Gary's
  mother
had from him, the busted marriage, the drug
  problems,
had sent her to an early grave. But it wasn't Gary's
  mother

I thought of as I listened but the basement where
    we spent
most of our afternoons one summer, the two of us
    and Helen,
Helen the only German Jew I knew, who'd come
    after the war
from someplace else, not Germany (though no one
    told me where),
to live with them, to be his nanny. He called her
    Zumzing
because she hardly spoke except to ask, every so
    often,
can I get you zumzing, Gary, you want zumzing
    now?
and whether he wanted anything or not he'd answer,
get me zumzing Zumzing, and laugh, so I'd laugh
    too.
Helen, though, unmindful of the teasing, or inured
    to it,
which made it easier to do, would hover over Gary,
her readiness to please him unassailable, yet
    strangely dour,
joyless, like someone on indefinite probation for
    some crime
nothing she could ever do could quite make up for.

•

Whenever he'd ask, she'd get the bottle Gary said
wasn't a bottle but a big cigar. Though eight years
    old,
he'd nuzzle against her, "smoking," gazing at
    nothing,
Helen stroking his hair, reminding him, Vee don't
    tell Mama,
dis just our secret, vee don't tell your mama now,
at which he'd pause, grinning, saying Vee dis, vee
    dat,
with the cigar held gangster style between his
    fingers.
It never occurred to me to make fun of him.
He'd look up from the bottle from time to time,
    and smile,
and seem so certain I'd admire him for this, I
    couldn't not.
It was as if in going down into the basement
he'd gone beyond the reach of how we usually were,
becoming at the same time both older and younger
than he should have been. It thrilled me, being there
with him, all the rules suspended, making new
    rules up,
the games that he'd want to play so like and unlike
the games I knew that to play them was to feel
myself complicit in the secrets he and Helen shared:

•

Whoever was "it" would be buried under cushions
and stay there dead while Helen counted to a hun-
        dred.
Then "it" would roar and rise and hunt the other
        down,
whipping him back into the pit where he'd be
        buried.
Or with the cushion Helen would wall in a corner of
        the basement,
and Gary and I would take turns guarding each
        other, marching
back and forth before the entrance, a rifle on one
        shoulder,
until the prisoner watching for the slightest lapse
would storm the gate, all of the cushions tumbling
down around us as we wrestled to the floor.


I remember reading of the children in the camps
        and ghettos,
how in their stubborn urge for pleasure where there
        was no pleasure
they'd pretend the horrors they were living through:
the bigger ones who got to be the Germans whip-
        ping and beating
the smaller ones who were the Jews, to dig their
        graves,
stage funerals, line each other up, and through it all,

German and Jew together, they would all be
    laughing.
During the war, wouldn't Helen have been about
    the age
that we were then? I wonder now what she was
    seeing,
or wanted to see as she looked on, waiting until the
    play
got too rough, as it always would, and one of us
    would cry
before she'd pull us off each other and, hugging Gary
or hurrying to get him out another bottle, ask
in the same flat tone, Now vee do zumzing else now,
    jah?
My mother didn't know where Helen was now,
or whether she went on living with the family
after Gary dropped out of high school and moved
    away.
She said it drove his mother crazy how she spoiled
    him rotten.
Did Helen mourn the trouble he got into? Or had she
by the time we knew her had her fill of mourning,
her heart by then concerned with other things,
    things he
unwittingly provided, Gary never more enslaved
than in the license she made him think was his?

    Could he have been her plaything too, as much as

she was his,
her puppet of a secret brooding on what couldn't be
    forgotten,
all of her life from the war on (and she was just a
    girl then)
a mere reprise, a deafening echo chamber?

And even now
I wonder who's obliging whom when Helen—
after all these years of never being thought of, lost
among the minor people of my personal history —
rises from the dead through small talk to become
my personal link to what I can't imagine.

It almost seems I have my way with her again,
seeing her there in the last scene, down on her knees
surrounded by a chaos of innumerable pieces
of the train set she's saying is like the one she played
    with
with her papa long ago, an aura of dread and
    urgency
about her as she hurries to put it all together,
    working
to keep us down there with her a little longer,
to keep us from going anywhere she wouldn't follow
(did I ever see her leave the house?): all over the
    basement,

the tracks in curves and straightaways, the signs for
    Stuttgart,
München, Würzburg, Berlin, the flashing signal
    lights,
the flagman in the switching yard, black-coated
    porter at the station,
and beyond it shops, cafés, and houses, a church and
    school—
the flanged wheels fitted to the tiny rails, and Gary
settled in her lap now, his hands on the black box
easing the lever as she whispers dis one, jah, now dat,
and the cars click forward through that miniature
    world.
Soon, though, bored, he throws the black box down,
    and he and I
rampage over everything, stomping and pulling it
    all apart
while Helen laughs (the only time I ever heard her
    laugh).

ALAN SHAPIRO is a poet and essayist who lives
in Chapel Hill, North Carolina. His most recent
book of poetry, *The Dead Alive and Busy,* was published by the University of Chicago Press.

# The Cone War

## *E. Ethelbert Miller*

I remember the Cone War the way I remember Bill Mazeroski touching third base after hitting his home run in the 1960 World Series. In the shadow of St. Margaret's Episcopal Church around the corner from Longwood Avenue in the Bronx, the older boys and girls gathered one summer afternoon. It was a hot day, the kind of day when you want to suck on ice and let some of the cold water drip down the front of your shirt. A few kids decided to ride their bikes down to the factories near the East River.

One of the factories made ice cream cones. On this particular summer day someone at the factory must have been sunstruck or just generous and gave about six kids several boxes of cones.

The bike riders came back to our block like World War II veterans from Europe. They had *cones, free cones!* The day stopped and everyone wanted one. We munched on some but soon decided the cones made wonderful projectiles so we divided them up and began throwing them around. Cones crashed against new haircuts and the battle soon engulfed the entire street.

We dashed between cars, up the steps of stoops, into hallways, laughing and dodging cones like the missiles Kennedy would warn us about. As the Cone War escalated a few kids tried to ride their bikes back to the factory for more supplies. One kid was intercepted as a cone splattered off the top of his head and he fell off his bike in the middle of the street. We laughed until our sides hurt and the sidewalks were filled with crumbs like nuclear fallout. This was during the days when we had air raid drills and signs that directed us to bomb shelters.

The Cone War must have lasted only twenty minutes but it became a memory like a folktale from a book. For one moment in my childhood a war became a moment of beautiful destruction and we did not die. Now the friendships are long gone but an empty cone reminds me of my lost youth and a summer day in the Bronx without ice cream.

E . ETHELBERT MILLER lives in Washington, D.C. He is the author of several collections of poems. Mr. Miller was awarded the 1995 O. B. Hardison, Jr., Poetry Prize. In 1996, he received an honorary doctorate of literature from Emory & Henry College. His most recent book is *Fathering Words: The Making of an African-American Writer.*

# Remember That Time

*Andrew Shue*

I am the man I am today because of the boy I was yesterday—no doubt about it.

If I didn't know that before, it hit me like a ton of bricks at 3:30 the morning after Michael Ristau's wedding. Michael was one of my best friends growing up. Over the years we remained close and I was a groomsman when he got married a few years ago. At the end of the reception, when everybody was danced out, we took refuge by the bar.

It was the perfect time to start telling some of the

stories of the things we had done, the games we invented, the sports we played as kids. I'm not talking about crazy stories from college—or even high school—I'm talking about the stories from when we were *kids.*

One of our favorites was the '73 World Series, the beloved Mets playing the hated A's right in my backyard in South Orange, New Jersey. Michael and I and our friends put up banners and wore Mets and A's uniforms (I was thirty-two, the same number as my favorite pitcher in the Mets rotation, Jon Matlack). We bought lime to mark the field so we would know exactly what was fair and what was foul. There were to be no "do-overs." This was serious.

When we were all lined up at the start of the game, I remember feeling *We're really playing the Major Leagues here.* My grandmother even came out, microphone in hand (really a wooden spoon), and belted out the "Star-Spangled Banner."

As happy as I was for Michael on the day of his wedding, I will always resent that he played for the A's. He also never lets me forget that I walked three batters in a row and started to cry.

I was only seven for the World Series, but I was nine when the Minnesota Vikings played the Pittsburgh Steelers in the Super Bowl—also in my back-yard.

I played for the Vikings and wore number 44—Chuck Foreman. My younger brother played center and wore number 53—Mick Tingelhoff. We still have those jerseys and while the colors may have faded, the memories are still vivid—breaking tackles and doing the Foreman "spin move" and making diving catches in the snow. Once again, my Vikings lost to Michael's Steelers.

In the wintertime when we weren't playing foot-ball, you could find us in the Greemans' driveway playing street hockey—sometimes instead of going to school. My parents got divorced when I was in the fifth grade, so my mom started to work. She would leave the house around 7:00 in the morning and it was up to us to go to school, so at least once a month we would stay home part of the day and play street hockey.

Our house didn't have a smooth pavement, so we would walk up the street and use the Greemans' driveway. We never even asked them: We would just show up and start playing. And why not? We were kids; we thought the whole neighborhood was our playground.

On the baseball field I was Jon Matlack, on the

football field I was Chuck Foreman, but on the Greemans' driveway, unless I was the goalie, I was Brian Trottier of the New York Islanders. After losing the World Series and the Super Bowl, it was great to win the Stanley Cup. This time it was against my younger brother John. I scored the winning goal, with only one second left. I can still hear my brother's call of the final moments: "5, 4, 3, Trottier shoots . . ."

We didn't just stage major sporting events, we also made up entire games. Roof Railers, Soccer Bat, Throw the Rotten Apple (that one only lasted an hour). The goal of Roof Railers was simple. We would climb atop every garage roof in the neighborhood. What I remember most is that, like all good games growing up, Roof Railers had enough danger to make it exciting.

Soccer Bat was less dangerous, but probably our best creation—it was part baseball, part stickball, and part dodge ball. The pitcher would bounce a soccer ball at the batter. The batter would swing a baseball bat and hit the ball. If the ball was caught you were out. If it was a grounder, those in the field would pick up the ball and whip it at the runner. Simple enough. We would play for hours.

Why was Soccer Bat our best creation? Because we

made it up. It was ours. In a way we were inventing our lives.

Thinking about Michael Ristau's wedding and reflecting on my adulthood, it's pretty clear how strong an influence those games we played had on me. Staging an elaborate World Series in our backyard and playing games like Roof Railers and Soccer Bat didn't just occupy my free time—it made me more creative, more interested in trying new things, more willing to take risks. Not only as a kid, but now. It was a real gift, that we had that time—that we didn't have a lot of structure, and that we had the freedom to play our own games and to grow up. But not too quickly.

ANDREW SHUE has competed in many games in several different fields. In the last ten years his thirst for new experiences has driven him to be a teacher, an actor, an athlete, a community leader, and an entrepreneur. Shue, who is a husband and the father of two, starred in FOX television's *Melrose Place* for six years and made his feature film debut in *The Rainmaker,* directed by Francis Ford Coppola.

# Keeping Up
# with Cal

*Billy Ripken*

We Ripkens are a baseball family, and the games we
Ripken kids played were baseball games. Not sur-
prisingly, Cal was the best.

When I was a kid, my family traveled around a
lot. Among the kids there was Elly, the oldest; Cal, a
year behind her; Fred, a year after that; and me, almost four and a half years younger than Cal. Every
summer we would pile into our blue Buick station
wagon and catch up with Dad, who was paying his
dues coaching in the minor leagues. Phoenix, Ari-

zona . . . Pensacola, Florida . . . Amarillo, Texas . . .
Asheville, North Carolina—we traveled around so
much that we were constantly leaving our friends behind. So we relied on each other for friendship and
fun. At the ballpark we would play to pass the time
until Dad was ready to go home. All kids like to
hang out at their dad's office; ours happened to be
the ballpark.

For Cal and me, creating a game of baseball was
simply a matter of finding the resources, and as kids
we were pretty resourceful. Leftover programs rolled
up tight made for a perfect bat; crushed red-and-
white Coca-Cola cups were our balls. But we needed
a lot of those since they turned to mush after a few
good whacks from Cal. For bases we used the tinfoil
wrappers from hotdogs.

Of course we weren't always at the ballpark.

During one season we lived in a small house in
North Carolina with a circular backyard and a small
stone wall all the way around it. There we had the
confines for a real field. A ball made of wadded white
athletic tape replaced the Coke cups, and a cut-off
broomstick served as the bat. Even back then, Cal
was better than the rest of us. I would throw that
tape ball as hard as I could, always with the same result—over the wall, down the hill, and across the

street (to find Cal's ball I'd go). For me, tape ball was largely about chasing.

When it was my turn to hit, I would choke way up on the bat just like Felix Millan—one of the players I got to see in the Southern League. I knew I couldn't do what Cal could do, so I was always trying to do what I saw the guys at the park doing. Cal, of course, never imitated anyone. I think that even back then he knew that he was going to be somebody the kids would emulate, so he could just be himself. But for me it was Felix Millan, who used to choke his hands halfway up the bat so he wouldn't strike out. When Cal would get two strikes on me, that's what I did, just hoping to make contact, just hoping to stay alive, just trying to compete with Cal.

If it was raining, we took the game indoors, where we always had one of those giveaway miniature Louisville Sluggers lying around. Inside, the pitcher would use Ping-Pong balls, but we didn't just lob the ball over the plate. There were Ping-Pong fast balls, curve balls, even knuckle hooks. Have you ever tried to hit a nasty breaking Ping-Pong ball with a twelve-inch baseball bat from less than six feet away? Cal could do it.

Making up games didn't stop with the end of childhood. After his 1980 AA league season in Charlotte, Cal brought home a variation called half ball. It wasn't very complicated. We took a rubber ball, cut it in half and headed outside, where we set up a folding chair behind the hitter that would represent the unarguable strike zone. If the ball hit the chair, it was a strike, as simple as that. Just like when we were playing with the Ping-Pong ball, Cal had some real nasty pitches. He would cup the uncut round side of the ball in his big right hand and lift his leg in an exaggerated windup, sometimes pausing for effect. He knew what was coming next. We both knew. It didn't matter. The exposed crinkled rubber would flutter through the air, passing literally centimeters from my neck before dropping and skimming the top of the chair. I would just stand there helpless. I couldn't say a word or blame the ump. It hit the chair. I'm out.

When Cal was at bat during our games, it was a replay of tape ball in North Carolina. I'd have to go around the neighbor's house and find the ball because he'd hit it to kingdom come. He kept hitting it farther and farther and I would just try throwing it harder and harder.

As futile as it seems, it was fun. All the games were fun, mostly because Cal took them to another level. That's probably why he is where he is and why he's going to the Hall of Fame. I'd like to think I played a little part. Cal Ripken could never have hit the ball over the wall, down the hill, and across the street—not without a pitcher.

BILLY RIPKEN played in the Major Leagues for eleven years—seven of them alongside his big brother Cal.

# What a Year

*George Stephanopoulos*

1969, what a year to be a kid in New York.

The same year I was playing football on Sundays with my friends in the sunken garden under the shadows of my dad's church, the Jets' Joe Namath was telling reporters, "We are going to win the Super Bowl." Broadway Joe didn't just predict it; he guaranteed it. And his statement made headlines around the country. I loved it.

1969, the same year my older sister was holding her own on the court with me and the guys, Walt "Clyde" Frazier, the crushed-velvet fedora wearing silky smooth basketball player, was beginning another New York championship run. Many recall the decisive seventh game at Madison Square Garden, Knicks versus the Lakers. That was the game when a hurt Willis Reed—the Knicks' leading scorer who had been sidelined with an injury—hobbled dramatically onto the court. But what most people forget is it was my hero, Clyde Frazier, who led the way to victory: thirty-six points, nineteen assists, and five steals. The game of a lifetime.

1969, the same year I played hockey in the gymnasium with an oversized plastic goalie stick in my right hand and a baseball glove in my left (we didn't have real hockey gloves), the Rangers were playing deep into the playoffs. Our gym didn't have "blue seats" like they did at the Garden, but that didn't stop me from pretending to be Eddie Giacomin, the Rangers' all-star goalie. After I made a sprawling kick save, I would chant to myself, "Ed-die! Ed-die!" The crowd goes crazy.

1969, the same year the New York Mets were such a big deal that teachers wheeled TVs into a classroom so we could watch the games, I forced myself to stay awake as Tom Seaver tried to pitch a perfect game and cried myself to sleep when he didn't. The same year the cellar dwellers became the Amazin' Mets, the same year that a group of overachievers—Koosman, Gentry, Agee, Jones—won the World Series, it was an undersized kid in Purchase, New York, who pulled off the *real* miracle. An unassisted triple play in kickball.

The kickball field was actually the school parking lot. In schoolbus yellow, there was a rectangle painted for the pitching mound, a square for home plate, and three diamonds for the bases. It wasn't exactly Shea Stadium, but for a game of kickball that's all we needed. That and one of those red rubber balls.

I was playing second base. Only a few second-graders in Purchase could throw the ball all the way from shortstop or third to first base. So the fact that I was playing second—only a few feet from the first base—was a pretty good sign I wasn't a real star. But on that day I was.

The bases were loaded and I was probably five steps to the left of second. Packy Morgan got up and drilled a line drive straight at me. I couldn't avoid it if I wanted to.

Got me right in the gut. I didn't drop it. One out.

As the kid on second bolted for third, I took a few steps over and stepped on second. Two outs.

Then Larry Fennell—the kid who thought he was so cool in his PF Flyers—broke for home. I rifled the ball and hit him on the butt. And that was it. That's a triple play in kickball.

1969. I'll never forget it.

GEORGE STEPHANOPOULOS, now a political analyst at ABC News, has retired his kickball Keds.

# The Craziest Kid in the World

## Brad Meltzer

We stood at the top of the stairs for what felt like an hour. Pacing. Watching. Craning our necks to see if he'd really do it.

"There's no way," one of us murmured.

"He's gotta be nuts," said another.

But John Chiarmonte, with his wild curly hair and his toothy grin of invulnerability, was determined to prove us wrong. When it comes to physical consequences, ten-year-olds never sweat a possible injury. It's like someone once said: You don't worry about falling out of a tree until they teach you about gravity in school.

In our case, we didn't know gravity. We knew John Chiarmonte. And for better or worse, he was about to jump down an entire flight of stairs. We were there to cheer him on.

"Youcandoit," I shouted.

His cousin, John Lucchese, patted him on the back. Anything to get him to go.

John Chiarmonte took another look down the long flight of stairs that led down to his basement. There had to be twenty to twenty-five steps in all— but more important, there wasn't a lot of running room for the windup, so if he planned to clear them all, it'd have to be a huge jump. The only problem was, if he jumped too high, he'd smack his head into the ceiling that covered the lower half of the staircase. To even the odds, we gave him one advantage— at the base of the stairs we dragged a thin, old, ratty mattress that we found in the back of the basement.

"Youcandoit," I repeated.

He nodded. It was gonna have to be a low and fast leap. A solid leap—John's stairs weren't carpeted. Like most basement stairs back then, they were lined with metal treads on the edge of each step.

It seemed so easy when it started: One of us

jumped down the last two steps of the staircase, another jumped from the third to the bottom, then the fourth. . . .

Now, John Chiarmonte stood at the top, and a thin, damp mattress waited for him at the bottom. Removing his glasses, he was ready to go. He was really going to do it. He *had* to do it—that was the only way to win the title, "Craziest Kid in the World."

To be honest, I'm not sure how the game actually started. As with all the best childhood games, we were always playing it—the champion changing from competition to competition. You couldn't blame your glove or your racket in "Craziest Kid in the World." In fact, the only thing this game required was guts, the possibility for glory, and at least one witness. It wasn't crazy unless someone saw it.

While I'm not sure *when* the game started, I do know when it peaked. Fourth grade, Brooklyn, 1980. Back then, we were too young for fashion (though we did love the fact that Lee Rosenberg used to wear Lee jeans) and too old to completely ignore the girls. As a result, every school day focused on two things: 1) impressing the ladies with witty repartee in their slam books; and 2) lunch.

And I'm not talking cafeteria lunch. In fourth

grade, in Brooklyn, if you had a note from your parents, you were allowed to leave the school grounds for lunch. It was a big deal. No supervision—the first step to adulthood. That's how it was on a normal day. A sunny day. But this day—this was a rainy day.

When it rained at P.S. 206, the schoolyard's drainage system always clogged, creating a huge puddle in the right field of our punchball court. So even though the rain eventually let up, the puddle was still there—a taunting obstacle to every one of us waiting to play ball, but a perfect setting for another round of "Craziest Kid in the World."

It started when a group of us made our way to examine the lakelike puddle. Maybe we wanted to see how deep it was; maybe we were just fascinated by how big it was. Either way, with fifteen minutes of lunch remaining, a small crowd of fourth-grade boys was standing on the edge of the puddle. Within seconds, we were daring each other to step toward the middle. That's all it took. A group of us on our own. No supervision. A clear obstacle. The game was on.

As always, John Chiarmonte was one of the first. After his gold medal in the Leap-Down-the-Stairs competition, he had nothing to prove. Yet, as we knew from Muhammad Ali, you can't quiet a champion.

Seconds after one of us took off his shoes and tube socks and ran along the edge of the puddle, John Chiarmonte stormed straight through the center—the conquering hero high-stepping his way to victory. His legs were soaked and his sneakers were sponges. Naturally, we cheered our heads off.

It was a great moment, a hysterical moment—but it wasn't destined to last.

Refusing to be outdone, Lee Rosenberg stepped forward and walked calmly into the center of the murky maw. Our mouths dropped open. He wasn't usually a player. Just seeing him out there. . . . It wasn't like he was breaking the rules; there were no rules—the field was everywhere, everyone was a possible player—but usually, we stuck to our scripted roles. When the game started, I knew my place: I was an instigator. And Lee, he was usually a spectator. But now, with a few minutes left for lunch, Lee Rosenberg was a player. A major player.

I can still see him strolling out into the middle of the puddle. The water came up to the calves of his dark jeans. His feet were lost. Watching our expressions and knowing he had us, he raised his arms in a giant "V" for Victory. Then, to make sure John Chiarmonte got the message, he put the cherry on top. In one quick movement, he sat down, smack in the center of the puddle—fully dressed and patting the water like a kid in a kiddie pool. With his legs straight in front of him, Lee just sat there. All we could see were the tips of his sneakers and the vanity tag of his Lee jeans.

Within seconds, we went nuts—screaming, shouting, and no doubt trying to egg the next player on. Lee had taken the title; you couldn't go back to class that soaked. So who would dare top this?

Ronnie. The new kid.

Whenever a new kid moved to school, he always seemed to be shy and quiet. Ronnie, however, was a kid who was clearly popular in whatever school he previously attended. And when he moved to our school, he wasn't going to take it sitting down—much less sitting down in a puddle.

We all knew that Ronnie was anxious to prove himself. But when the five-minute bell sounded through the schoolyard, we knew time was running out.

Thanks to Lee, the crowd had grown—a four-foot mob now surrounded the puddle. So for the new kid, it was now or never. The title was his to take, but it had to be something no one could top. Indeed, that was how the game was always played. As the time ticked down, the one-upmanship got exponential.

The dares got wilder. If you wanted to be the Craziest Kid in the World, you had to take a chance.

And so, as we all looked on, Ronnie did the unthinkable. It was like throwing the Hail Mary of insanity. He ran over to the metal grate that covered the main drain in the concrete and slid his fingers through the metal bars. With a quick tug, he pulled the grate off. We were chocolate pudding in his hands. And in one triumphant splash, Ronnie stuck his entire head into the filthy muck of the backed-up sewer.

The crowd, as expected, went wild.

But when he pulled his head out—after shaking off the water like a wet dog and rubbing the dirt from his face—Ronnie realized that the crowd had suddenly gone silent. The cheers had stopped. Our eyes were wide with terror.

"What?" Ronnie asked, even though he was starting to feel the answer.

It must've been getting harder for him to see. As he wiped off his face, his eyes were almost completely swollen shut. They looked like two puffed-up red grapes. Whatever was in that sewer . . . something was clearly wrong.

At that moment, the late bell sounded. Except for three of us, the entire mob took off—rats on our sinking ship. Later, they'd all be able to say they didn't want to be late for class.

"What do I do?" Ronnie shouted to those of us who remained. His hands were shaking; he was on the verge of tears. We stood there in silence. All you could hear was the dripping from Lee's Lees.

"Go home," we decided. "You gotta get your mom." The solution to every fourth-grade problem.

He turned around and ran—hysterical and as fast as he could—out the back gate of the schoolyard.

Even at ten years old, there's a fine line between crazy and stupid, and as the rest of us ran back to class, we knew we'd crossed it. As long as Ronnie kept his head in that sewer, he was a hero. When he pulled it out . . . "Craziest Kid in the World" was over.

BRAD MELTZER lives in Maryland and writes novels, including *The Tenth Justice, Dead Even,* and his newest book, *The First Counsel.* Today, John Chiarmonte is a DJ for Flashdancers, an X-rated strip club in New York City. No one knows where Ronnie is.

# Wild Child

## *Jackie Collins*

When I was thirteen I decided that school bored the hell out of me, my fellow classmates were babies, and it occurred to me that it was definitely time I livened things up. I'd already been making up scurrilous stories that I wrote in my diary and sold for a few pence a shot. But sales were not what they used to be, and I suspected that my tales of liaisons with strapping teenage boys from the high school down the street were wearing thin. Naïve young girls were beginning to question me. Was it *really* possible that I could sneak out to a discotheque until 1:00 A.M. without my parents finding out? Actually, yes, because my family lived in a basement apartment around the corner from Baker Street; being a total wild child I was able to climb out of my bedroom window and vanish into the night, leaving several pillows stuffed under the covers, so if anyone should check up on me it looked like I was in bed asleep.

Oh, the adventures I experienced! Thank goodness I was street smart at a very early age and knew how to ward off randy strangers who had no idea I was only thirteen. Fortunately I looked at least eighteen in my short skirts and tight sweaters—borrowed from my big sister, Joan, who had been whisked off to Hollywood by Twentieth Century-Fox to pursue a career as a movie star. Lucky her. Hollywood was my dream— I worshipped Rock Hudson and adored the darkly handsome Tony Curtis. In fact, I had fan photos of movie stars plastered all over my bedroom walls.

So there I was, stuck in London at school, from which I managed to play truant three days a week, and very, very bored. Until one exciting day, along came a new student. Her name was Barbara and she was an American who was somewhat behind in her grades. So, fortunately for me, she joined my class, even though at fifteen she was two years older than everyone else.

Ah . . . fifteen . . . what a magical age. I envied her

immediately, and once she realized how lame the other girls were, we bonded. Great. Finally I had a playmate who understood me and my somewhat quirky, overactive imagination.

"What's your story?" she asked me one day.

Story? Hmm . . . story. . . .

"I'm really American," I confessed, lying quickly. "My dad is an undercover agent for the CIA, and here's the thing—we're living in England because he's tracking a notorious criminal who's out to blow up the world."

Barbara raised a cynical eyebrow but did not say a word.

"You cannot tell a soul," I added. "What I've just told you is top secret."

Barbara nodded. She knew a good story when she heard one, especially a story concerning secrets. "*My dad's in the witness protection program,*" she informed me, casually tossing back her lustrous jet-black hair. "We used to live in New York but it got too dangerous. They had to move us."

I nodded, believing every word. And after that we became firm friends.

Barbara was the best thing that ever happened to me. She taught me how to apply makeup, wear high heels (filched from her mother's closet), flirt outrageously with any poor male who glanced in our direction, and sneak into movies for free. We both loved movies and thought nothing of skipping school and cruising the West End of London, where there were lots of movie theaters. She was as crazy about Rock Hudson as I was (if only we'd known!), and we both adored Ava Gardner, with her smoldering eyes and luscious lips, not to mention her notorious love life. Then there were James Dean, Marlon, Natalie. . . .

Barbara and I could've lived at the movies, and we practically did. Until one afternoon, strolling casually across Piccadilly Circus on our way from one cinema to another, we were stopped by a couple of cops—one male, one female. Barbara didn't hesitate—without stopping a beat she ran, zooming off down Shaftesbury Avenue with not a backward glance.

I was shocked, and so were the two cops, who grabbed my arm and held on lest I should run too.

"What have you two girls been up to?" questioned the male cop.

"How old are you?" demanded the female.

I watched in horrified fascination as Barbara vanished into the distance. My pal. My comrade. So much for loyalty. She'd totally dumped on me and I couldn't believe it.

"I'm American," I blurted.

"We don't care about your nationality," said the female cop. "We want your age."

"Sixteen," I muttered.

"I don't think so," said the woman, not fooled by my bright pink lipstick and curve-hugging sweater. "Looks to me like you should be in school instead of hanging around the West End."

"I'm sixteen," I repeated defiantly. "I've left school."

"Well then," she said, staring at me disbelievingly, "let's phone your mum and check that out. What's your name?" she added, producing an official-looking notebook.

Panic overcame me. Why hadn't I run, too? I could just imagine my mother's face if she got a call from a policewoman saying I'd been caught loitering in a bad area when she thought I was safely in school. And my father would have a heart attack.

"Jill," I muttered, using my middle name in hopes that it would somehow help me get out of this mess.

"And your parents' phone number?"

"Please!" I gasped "Don't call them, they'll be furious."

"Playing truant, huh?" said the male cop.

I nodded miserably.

"Not sixteen, right?" said the female cop with a knowing sneer.

I nodded again. "Please," I begged. "Let me off this time. I promise I'll never do it again."

The two cops conferred. By this time my swagger was failing and I dreaded the punishment my parents would no doubt hand out.

Finally the male cop spoke. "You're playing a dangerous game," he said warningly. "Pretty young girl like you could get in a lot of trouble walking these streets."

"I wasn't walking these streets," I objected. "I was on my way to the Underground."

"Okay," said the female cop. "We'll take you to your train and put you on it. But if we ever see you around here again. . . ."

Whew! Narrow escape.

I didn't play truant for another month. And I never spoke to Barbara again.

She was expelled shortly after, and two years later so was I. No big deal. School had always bored the hell out of me.

But I'll always remember the games. . . .

JACKIE COLLINS is the author of seventeen provocative and controversial international bestsellers. She lives in Beverly Hills.

# The Walk

*Lou Stovall*

You can be sure there was no time in my life when being cool was more important than it was my first year of high school. Being cool was the most serious game I ever played.

Cool is a state of being; embracing the elusive elements of the right walk, talk, stance, attitude, look, and belief. If you do not truly believe that you are cool, then you are truly uncool. In high school I had to believe in myself, and I believed that I was a chunk of ice. I truly believed that I was cool.

The walk was everything. Something between a slide and glide, without skates, and a little hitch to the left or right. Add a bit of swagger—just a bit, too much looks silly if not totally stupid.

So there I was—my walk was hip, I was cool, and I was headed for high school. At fourteen, life was sweet.

LOU STOVALL is an artist and master printmaker who has worked with such artists as Jacob Lawrence, Sam Gilliam, and Joseph Albers. For more than thirty years he has taught his craft and helped build a community of artists in Washington, D.C.

# Chinaberry War

**Ken Wells**

I grew up in a little place called Bayou Black below
New Orleans deep in south Louisiana's Cajun Belt.
We lived on a farm across the road from the bayou on
about six acres, which was a good number since I was
one of six boys. A boy an acre seemed about the right
ratio for my father, who liked his sons, but not un-
derfoot. Sometimes my mother on rainy days, which
are common in that humid, swampy place, longed
for a six-acre house instead of the tight, tin-roofed
cypress colonial that we shared with our grandparents, Momma and Pop Wells.

When the weather was good, though, my mother

did not need to worry. For the farm not only consisted of six acres, but it had a rickety old barn to hide out in and lots of hutches and coops and pens for the Wells menagerie—quail, ducks, chickens, rabbits, snakes, a pig named Petunia, a ram named Sylvester, a monkey named Peanut. And then there was a wild mink named Stinky who had survived a run-in with my father's Jeep station wagon one foggy morning and recovered so heroically that he was spared the skinning knife. Our seven dogs and numerous feral cats had the run of the place, and Henrietta, our milk cow, was queen of the back barbed-wire pasture.

We were also spared the distraction of immediate neighbors. The Daigles lived about a half mile up the bayou and the Schexnayders about a mile down. In between stood hundreds of acres of sugar cane (and a bit of corn). Before they were mowed down during the annual sugar cane harvest (an event known as grinding), the cane fields—together with the barn, the cow pasture, the corn crib, and the jungly, overgrown bayouside—were the scenes of epic skirmishes in our longest-running childhood game.

We called it Chinaberry War.

The inspiration for Chinaberry War and the source of its armaments grew on the west side of the house:

Sprawling out of control, the chinaberry tree was just one of several miraculous trees on our farm. On the verge of the back pasture stood a tall cottonwood ideal for climbing (and pretending you were a lookout aboard Jean Lafitte's pirate ship). On the east side of our yard, near our saggy cypress garage, sat an arbor of fig trees drooping every summer with the sweet, sticky fruit (so many figs, in fact, that we picked them and sold them in gallon buckets from an impromptu roadside stand). Off the back porch, over by the clothesline, grew a small bay tree from which my mother could pluck and dry bay leaves for her next gumbo. Fronting the house were tangerine, orange, and grapefruit trees that swayed with golden citrus each fall. On the west side, off the front porch, stood an impressive hackberry—a tree with a trunk so brambly and boughs so thick that it discouraged even the Wells boys from climbing it except on a dare. ("Climbing a hackberry," Pop Wells used to say, "is like climbing into a nest of scratching cats.")

But best of all, we had, between the hackberry and our corn crib, the splendid chinaberry tree.

The chinaberry is exotic to that exotic part of the world. It was not a particularly good climbing tree, lacking the low-hanging handholds of the cottonwood that made it easy for even a short boy to get purchase, and its branches were a bit too spindly to hold much weight. But each spring and summer it produced hard, green, sour fruit about the size of a marble, inedible except to unparticular birds but perfect for putting in a slingshot and going after birds—or your brothers.

Birds, we learned, were a lot easier to fell with BB guns. But boys made big targets.

Chinaberry War was simple, as all the best games are. We'd break into teams, usually three boys in each team, usually just us brothers. We'd set the battlefield: For example, in bounds included the barn, the cow pasture, and the cane field beyond the pasture, clear to a grassy tractor road about a quarter of a mile away. The front yard, side yards, rear chicken pen—all places potentially visible to nosy parents looking out a window—were out of bounds. My mother hated all roughhouse games because boys sometimes got hurt or they led boys into actual combat—well, inept fistfights. My father, a Marine in the Big War, had lost his appetite for fighting of any kind, and anyway, he knew that a chinaberry fired hard from a slingshot would not be good for a boy struck in the eye.

Of course, this mild defiance of our parents' concerns, not to mention the chance of getting caught, made the game all the more *dangerous* and thus all the more alluring.

Once the teams were chosen, the game would start. One team would go off into the combat zone to hide; the other team—the one that drew the short stick—would camp up on the front or back porch, counting to one hundred very slowly and trying to keep the promise of not peeking as the other army melted into the field. During this time you could also plot strategy, which usually involved trying to guess where the blackguards would hide and try to ambush you.

The point was to ding your opponents with chinaberries. The rules firmly stated you were to aim below the belt—three hits and you were dead. Everybody was required to raise the Boy Scout salute, pledging to die at the appropriate time. This was sometimes a hard rule to follow, especially in the heat of combat. Everyone knew there was a risk of being smacked with high, errant chinaberries. This was *war,* after all.

Picking teams, however, sometimes proved problematic. Oh, it was simple to divide the available boys by size and comparative ability. A popular and fair combination involved oldest brother (Bill), fourth brother (Jerry), youngest brother (Bobby), against second brother (me), third brother (Pershing), fifth brother (Chris). It was a lot harder to convince the attacking team to also take on the mantle of some detested enemy. But good guys didn't go to war against each other; somebody had to be the bad guys.

There was, of course, a tradition of warriors in our family. My father had come back from World War II with numerous campaign ribbons and a purple heart (a shrapnel wound) after fighting in some of the great hellholes of the Pacific. On my mother's side, we had a great-great-grandfather who, along with his brother, fought for the Confederacy at Vicksburg in one of the pivotal battles of the Civil War. Both had been captured and held prisoner for several months. If being a Japanese soldier was unthinkable, being a Yankee soldier was also totally out of the question. So we had to pretty much settle on cowboys and Indians or a derivation, frontiersmen and Indians.

Davy Crockett and Daniel Boone were both on that fairly new contraption called the TV, as were our other heroes, Roy Rogers, Hopalong Cassidy, and the Lone Ranger. Of course, the Lone Ranger had his faithful sidekick Tonto, and who couldn't like Tonto? And I'd already read *The Last of the Mohicans* by James Fenimore Cooper and come to the shocking realization that there might be more to the Indian question than the scalp-stealing, brutal stereotypes who war-whooped through those much-beloved cowboy movies we saw down at the Bijou Theater in Houma.

So if your side got stuck being the attackers, you could at least pick some heroic tribe like the Sioux or Cheyenne and give yourself a name like Geronimo or Crazy Horse (but not Sitting Bull, which seemed like a dumb name for a warrior) and fly into battle, slingshot cocked, in full war cry.

I realize now that one of the unrecognized pleasures of growing up in the country back then was the ability to extend childhood in unconventional ways. Since we had no idea what adolescent boys were *supposed* to be doing, except maybe playing ball, fishing, and hunting, we felt free to do as we pleased—to invent our own games, like Chinaberry War. TV was barely considered entertainment, much less a cultural force (we caught two stations in black and white; reception was iffy on many days and switching from one channel to the next often required not just a turn of the channel knob but a trip outside to twist the TV antenna as well). Fashion standards, such as they were at Bayou Black School, were set by thrifty parents who depended on the Montgomery Ward catalogue to deliver sturdy shoes and blue jeans rugged enough to withstand the rigors of recess ball games and generic roughhousing. Peer pressure was diffuse. After school, kids went home to farms and chores and homework, and, if there was time, a dip in the bayou, a quick paddle in the pirogue, a quick game of baseball or football in the fading light. Nobody knew what cool or uncool was. You could be a full-fledged teenager and still indulge in child's play.

Which explains why on a warm, bright, sunny day at the age of fourteen going on fifteen, I have transformed myself into an attacking Indian and completed what I consider to be a brilliant feinting action, appearing on the edge of our pasture in full view of the barn. This is where I figure the cavalry (my brothers Bill, Jerry, and Bobby) will be maybe hiding behind hay bales or camouflaged under a mound of loose straw, waiting to pick me off as I enter the barn's cool dimness. But, having shown myself, I then disappear into a patch of uncut milkweed and Johnson grass, slithering between the pigpen and the chicken coop and doubling back to the side yard. Then, using the corn crib as a shield, I run as fast as my legs will take me toward the shelter of the cane field that runs up along the west side of the pasture, separated only by a grassy tractor road. The plan is to run unconcealed to a point even with the top of the pasture, then leave the field and slip under the barbed-wire fence *above* the barn.

They will be looking for me to attack from the south; I'll be slipping in from the north.

Better still, I have ordered my teammates, my two younger brothers, Pershing and Chris, to draw the cavalry out of the barn by showing themselves and ambling toward the barn door. Sometimes the enemy has been known to leap out en masse and try a kind of suicide attack; if they do it this time, I'll mow 'em all down from the rear. This seems like extremely clever strategy.

Luck seems to be on my side, for as I slide under the uppermost barbed-wire fence, there is Henrietta the cow. She's a docile milk cow, not quite as dumb as an ox, not quite as stubborn as a mule. So I sidle up to Henrietta and give her a friendly slap on the flank and a push at the neck. The idea is to herd Henrietta toward the barn, using her as cover until I am close enough to break off for my counterattack.

Henrietta cooperates admirably and my plan actually seems to be working. Bill and his team show

themselves and go after my younger brothers, who turn tail and run. Giving a war whoop, I peel off from Henrietta and go after them. I have a bead on Bobby, the easiest one to catch, when a terrible thing happens.

The rubber sling on my slingshot snaps in two. I have my free hand and pockets stuffed with chinaberries, but I am suddenly weaponless.

My whoop having given me away, the enemy has turned to confront me. I am suddenly surrounded, and chinaberries come whipping in from all directions. I dodge and plunge toward my attackers. I take a hit on the cheek, another on the arm, but these don't technically count since they are above the waist. They also sting like wasps.

I break for the house amid a chorus of shouts that I have been blasted many times below the waist and that I am already dead.

"Am not!" I yell.

"Are too!" they yell back.

I'm flying as fast as I can toward the house. I hear the thunder of cavalry behind me. When I reach the corn crib, I see my brother warriors waiting there for me. We turn and take our stand.

I cock my arm and blast the approaching mob with a handful of chinaberries at close range. This is also against the rules.

People are hit and yowling.

Somehow, we're all down together in a scrum of fists and elbows and yelps and kicks. Bill, being the biggest, manages to land on top. I end up on the bottom.

Then the screen door slams. There is my father.

"Break it up," he barks, "before somebody gets hurt!"

My father is medium tall, six foot or so in his stocking feet, but he has a way of pulling himself up that makes him look a lot taller. Up on the back-door steps, he looms like a giant.

We pull ourselves up off the ground, launching an intense six-sided debate about who cheated, who died, who shot high. Bill pushes; I push back. Other brothers crowd in. Rage rises. We are about to go at it full bore.

But my father quiets the mob with a shout that would fell a mule: "Knock it off, I said! And I don't want to have to tell you boys again!"

The heat has just been blasted out of us. We know *that* voice.

It would be extremely bad form to require our father to tell us again, for he has a way of devising diabolically clever punishments to remind us of the gravity and cost of our crimes. He has been known, for example, to send boys out to pick a long row of okra (extremely prickly to the touch) in the very hottest part of a summer day. You go with a uniform—heavy boots, heavy jeans, long-sleeved shirt, gloves, and hat—and you go with a bucket of a certain size that must be filled before you are readmitted to the family.

No, we've been busted, so we untangle our knot and head off in more or less different directions to cool off and nurse our intense grudges. I go down to the bayou, where my father has built a dock and a diving board, and watch minnows and water bugs skittering in the shallows.

A half-hour later, my anger is no longer boiling. It's on low, low simmer when I see Bill coming over the road toward the bayou carrying a baseball and a posthole digger.

"Whatcha doin'?" he says.

I'm still not sure I wanna talk to him yet but I speak up anyway.

"Uh, nothin'. Why?"

"I got a new game. Wanna play?"

"What is it?"

"Golf," he says.

I perk up. "Golf? You've found some golf clubs?"

"No, look. I've got Pop's posthole digger. We'll dig us a nine-hole course. We'll use a bat for our clubs and a baseball for the ball."

In about an hour, we've laid out our course, gotten out the lawnmower and mowed the "greens," flooded a ditch to make a water hazard, and laid down the rules: For tee and approach shots, you can toss the ball into the air and whack it, but once you're on the green, you have to putt, just like on a real golf course. You can play the ball from the rough or take a stroke and play it from the fairway.

And, if you hit your ball in Sylvester the ram's pen, you have to fetch it before he eats it, or suffer a five-stroke penalty.

This ends up becoming a brilliant rule, for Sylvester is a mean cuss and any boy who enters his lair will be chased and, if caught, butted.

We realize we have invented the perfect game—golf, with an element of the rodeo. Golf with an element of *danger!*

KEN WELLS is a features editor and writer for Page One of *The Wall Street Journal;* his debut novel, *Meely LaBauve,* about a boy growing up in the swamps of Louisiana, was published in spring 2000.

# Alley Cats

*Lisa Page*

Summertime was when the world opened its mouth wide and swallowed you whole. The sun beat down so that the tar went soft beneath your sandals, the grass sang at dusk, full of insects, and the trees rustled above your head. You were delicious, perched on the handlebars of your sister's bicycle, wind in your ears, careening up and down city streets, or poised on your skateboard, clackety clack, clackety clack.

Sometimes you were barefoot and careful—step on a crack, break your mother's back—in love with fresh-mowed grass and red clover, cottonwood seeds that turned the gutters white, mulberry bushes that stained the sidewalks blue, sprinklers that sprayed your feet along with the lawn and the pavement. Impervious to the heat, you felt that you'd died and gone to heaven because there was no homework, no crossing guard, no milk money in your shoe to worry about. You were intoxicated with the smell of suntan lotion mixed with car exhaust and smoke from barbecue pits.

Breathing in the scent of the lake on a breeze before a rainstorm. Catching lightning bugs as the sun went down, or grasshoppers in the middle of the day, which spat nasty brown juice in your hand. Smacking mosquitoes. Poking pillbugs with a twig so that they curled up in front of you and went round as stones. Savoring the snap of a jumprope, the thump of a basketball, the cars weaving in and out of the intersection on Fifty-fifth Street, windows rolled down and radios playing. If you were anything like my sister and me you ruled the streets. Specifically, you ruled Park Place, the street behind our townhouse development on the south side of Chicago.

Park Place was one of the newer streets in Hyde Park, built in 1960. You would call it a parking lot today, but for us it was a playground with a smooth blacktop, ideal for ball games. We played Dodge Ball and Elimination, Running Bases and Spud. Chinese Jumprope. Hopscotch. Cat's Cradle. Freeze Tag. We rode skateboards, radio flyers, roller skates, and bicycles with training wheels along Park Place. We climbed the surrounding fences, walls, trees, and swingsets, scraped our knees and nicked our elbows, suffered bee stings and mosquito bites—with relish. Because in those days, we were free. Fearless. Two little girls in the streets from morning till night, playing with the neighborhood kids, mostly boys. Domingo. Keith. Adam and Briar. Gamal (a girl who sometimes played rough the way we did). The Hyashi brothers. The Adache boys.

But there were weeks when the neighborhood went quiet. Hyde Park was home to the University of Chicago and for stretches of time the place emptied out. Families went to summer homes in Michigan or to visit extended family down South. The streets were dead, sunstruck and vast, drooping flowers tended by the occasional graduate student, house sitters here and there appearing with watering cans, emptying mail boxes, walking dogs. We were left to our own devices with no other children in sight. Two pitiful brown-skinned little girls in cut-offs and flip-flops, we dragged ourselves from door to door, knocking loudly or pressing door bells in vain. What would you have done? Retreated to the living room

and the TV set and watched soap operas all day? Pulled out the Barbie Dreamhouse and your Barbie dolls? Hauled out Monopoly and Parcheesi and Ouija? Yes indeed.

But you'd have gotten restless too, cooped up in the house with your mother and your baby brother, bored to death sipping lemonade, hungry for action. So you would head outside again, your sister beside you, determined to entertain yourself for real. You needed new territory, away from your mother's garden with its yellow fence and red geraniums.

Park Place stretched out, full of cars parked between yellow stripes, ivy climbing up the brick walls
of the townhouses, white butterflies fluttering
around your head. You knew where you were going.
Park Place fed into the alley that went beyond the
townhouse development all the way to Fifty-seventh
Street. You knew that alley like the back of your
hand, knew the texture of the tarpaper roofs on the
garages, the black shade of the gangways, the
chipped paint on the drainpipes.

Just weeks before, you hid there with a water bal-
loon slippery in your hand, waiting to slam it into
some poor unsuspecting boy's shoulder. You were an
alley cat, stepping over the different grades of pavement, where the blacktop turned to asphalt and the
asphalt to cobblestone.

The alley was a conduit to the past; like much of
Hyde Park, it was constructed for the Columbian Ex-
position of 1893. And the houses that lined it were
Victorian wood frames, or brick apartment buildings, Tudors, and brownstones. The backs of those
houses had latched wooden gates, garage doors and
padlocks, garbage cans, oil drums. Graffiti marked
up the walls and telephone poles stood tall as trees.
Weeds grew in the cracks beneath your feet, and
walking on them turned your feet green. Broken
glass glittered in the afternoon sun.

You were at Fifty-sixth Street by then, where the high-rise towered over you with windows like eyes. Its loading dock jutted into the alley like a boat, you thought. As you climbed the steps of the loading dock and surveyed the pavement below you told your sister you were deep sea divers and this was your treasure ship. And the pavement was water, with its curving green cracks and multicolored stones. You didn't need a treasure map, diving off the loading dock into the waves, gulping air, and then submerging again. White shards of glass were diamonds, red chips were rubies, green pieces emeralds. Brown and blue glass were amber and sapphires, bottle caps were gold bullion. Deep underwater there was other treasure, too: old batteries, stray marbles, cigarette butts. You sifted through gravel, twigs, seeds and stones, broken wire. You found razor blades, dog droppings, the occasional bone picked clean, ant hills, gum wrappers. Your booty was deposited into a rusted can, also rescued from the sea. But in between diving, sorting, and swimming, you had to wrestle a sea monster or two, fend off pirates (in the form of cars cutting through the alley on their way to Fifty-seventh Street), and avoid jagged rocks and poisonous seaweed.

And so you salvaged that particular summer day. You went home happy, your sister squinting in the late afternoon sun, pockets bulging with broken glass and a banged-up soup can full of trash in your hand. The alley rolled into Park Place again. The catalpas rustled above your head, seedpods dripping from their branches like green icicles. And you knew there was more treasure in store for you inside all the summer days yet to come.

LISA PAGE is a writer whose work has appeared in *Emerge, Playboy,* and *The Chicago Tribune.* Her essay "High Yellow White Trash" is included in the anthology *Skin Deep: Black Women and White Women Write About Race.* She lives with her family in Takoma Park, Maryland.

# Rocket Ball

## George Plimpton

I don't remember if the game we played had a name
(as in "let's go out and play catch"), though it did in-
volve an orange rubber ball, as I recall, the forebear of
the stickball spandau. Two other implements were
necessary—a three-legged iron stand (about the size
of football's kicking tee) and a cherry bomb, in mili-
tary nomenclature the infamous "M-80." I should
hastily add that when I was growing up fireworks
were legal in my state, and a good supply of cherry
bombs was a staple part of what one ordered from a
catalogue for the Fourth of July celebrations. These
cherry-sized firecrackers with their stiff inch-and-a-

half-long fuses have been outlawed for many years and with good reason, given their potential for boundless destruction to every part of the human anatomy, fingers in particular. But then they were legal, much to the despair of the family pets, who hid under beds for a week or so and were rarely seen until the cherry bomb supply ran out. Even then for a day or so they looked spooked, as if a dreadful detonation would go off when least expected, from behind the piano, perhaps.

The mechanics of the game were simple enough. Out on the lawn we set up the ball between the flanges of the iron stand, with the cherry bomb nestled in the grass directly underneath, placed so the fuse stuck out and could be ignited off a stick of punk.

That was exciting enough—to crouch down, blow on the end of the punk to get its tip glowing, and then touch it to the fuse, probing until the fuse ignited with a slight hiss.

When the cherry bomb went off a couple of seconds later, the thrust of the explosion shot the rubber ball to an extraordinary height, far loftier than any fungo, beyond any ball hit with a tennis racquet, a mere speck against the sky. The idea of the game was to try to catch the ball when it ultimately came hurtling back down . . . in our imaginations, playing shortstop for the Brooklyn Dodgers, the New York Giants, whichever, the bases loaded in the ninth, two men out, the team ahead by a run.

But the catch was secondary to the process of sending the ball to such an awesome height. I remember Robert Frost once hankered to do a poem about a fungo ball hit so far that it escaped the atmosphere and floated round and around the earth like a tiny moon—this in his earlier days, in fact an idea he had long before the scientists actually put a satellite into orbit. I like to think if he had seen our little rubber ball soar up over the house top, barely visible at its apex, he would have put himself to it. He once boasted that he could write anywhere, even with the back of a shoe as a writing board. In my mind's eye I see him standing at the porch's screen door. He comes out. He sits down in the grass and removes a sneaker. He extracts a piece of paper and a pencil from a shirt pocket. He looks at me and says, "Send that rubber ball up just once again, if you please."

GEORGE PLIMPTON, the originator of "participatory journalism," is the editor of *The Paris Review.* His books include *Paper Lion, Out of My League, The*

*Bogey Man, Open Net, The Curious Case of Sidd Finch, The X-Factor,* and most recently, *Truman Capote: In Which Various Friends, Enemies, Acquaintances, and Detractors Recall His Turbulent Career.*

# An Idyllic Childhood

## Hillary Rodham Clinton

I was born in Chicago, but when I was about four, I moved to where I grew up, which was Park Ridge, Illinois. It was your typical 1950s suburb. Big elm trees lined the streets, meeting across the top like a cathedral. Doors were left open, with kids running in and out of every house in the neighborhood.

We had a well-organized kid's society and we had all kinds of games, playing hard every day after school, every weekend, and from dawn until our parents made us come in at dark in the summertime.

One game was called chase and run, which was a kind of complex team-based hide-and-seek and tag combination. We would make up teams and disperse throughout the entire neighborhood for maybe a two- or three-block area, designating safe places that you could get to if somebody was chasing you. There were also ways of breaking the hold of a tag so that you could get back in the game. As with all of our games, the rules were elaborate and they were hammered out in long consultations on street corners. It was how we spent countless hours.

We also played softball, kickball, baseball—all on the corner, using the sewer tops for our bases. As we got older and could hit farther, we could no longer play there—we'd have to go to a playground. But probably until I was ten, that was all part of the fabric of our lives.

I played all the boys' games because I was kind of a tomboy and I had two younger brothers, and we had many, many more boys in our neighborhood than we had girls. I was a good baseball player, I was a good kickball player, I was a good tether ball player. I had a lot of interest in playing because I could play well enough to play with the boys.

We played most of our games in the streets, in backyards, and in the alleys. We had these alleys that were not big enough for a car to go down—our parents used them to put out the trash and to store things—and we used them as a narrow playing field.

In the summertime we would often go to the local swimming pool, the Hinckley Pool. It was unheated, the coldest water you've ever been in. I spent almost every summer afternoon of my young life in that pool.

In 1956 we organized our own neighborhood Olympics. I went to the dime store and I bought ribbons and we made medals. The kids organized all of these activities and contests in our streets and in our yards. We even broke up into different age groups. We set up the events, ran the events, and we even kept track of records that we set.

In fact, each contestant had to pay money to enter the neighborhood Olympics. At the end of the Olympics we had a big bag of pennies and nickels and quarters, which we gave to a local charity. I remember that because there was a picture of me in our local newspaper handing the bag of change to a man in a suit.

We were always playing some kind of sport. Our neighbors next door, the Williamses, always flooded their backyard so we could skate and play hockey and all kinds of winter sports. And then, of course, there were big skating rinks up at the parks and in back of our school, so we would always be going to those.

Most of the garages had basketball hoops so we would play a lot of Horse and Pig and one-on-one basketball. I spent a lot of time practicing my basketball shots. I also played basketball in high school—half-court basketball, because, back then, girls couldn't play full-court basketball. But I went to a school system that had great physical education programs: lacrosse, gymnastics, and field hockey. I've even done water ballet. I did it all. And now I think kids don't have that in a lot of their schools.

When my brother Hugh and I were little—I was probably five, so he was just two, we played in the basement. I made an elaborate space console, and we would go down in the basement and we'd take space trips. To this day he says that he was warped for life because one time I threw him out of the space ship and left him floating in space, and told him he couldn't come up to lunch because he was lost somewhere around Mercury.

We had so much imaginative game-playing time—just unstructured fun time. I had the best, most wonderful childhood: being outside, playing with my friends, being on my own, just loving life. When I was a kid in grade school, it was great. We were so independent, we were given so much freedom. But now it's impossible to imagine giving that to a child today. It's one of the great losses as a society. But I'm hopeful that we can regain the joy and experience of free play and neighborhood games that were taken for granted growing up in my generation. That would be one of the best gifts we could give our children.

HILLARY RODHAM CLINTON was first lady of the United States for eight years and is now a United States Senator from New York.

# You Can Take the Kid Out of New York

## Rob Reiner

I'm a fifty-three-year-old man. For the past twenty-five years, I have lived in Los Angeles and I've made my career working in Hollywood. And it has been a good life. But truth is, nothing compares with being a kid and growing up in New York. Luckily, since I work in a town of make believe, reliving that experience sometimes is only a movie set away.

As a young writer, my partner, Phil Michigan, and

I would walk around the Warner Brothers lot and head straight for the New York street. The buildings may have been fake, but the stoops were real enough. And if they weren't filming, we'd start playing— playing the games we grew up on.

With the Spaldeen in hand, it's the 1950s in the Bronx all over again. . . . The Spaldeen was the linchpin for almost everything we did. A 15 cent pink rubber ball made by the Spalding Company, the Spaldeen was perhaps the greatest ball every made. Imagination and a Spaldeen could keep you occupied forever. Let me demonstrate.

For stickball, all you needed was a broom handle for a bat, the Spaldeen, a bunch of guys, and a street. Manhole covers and parked cars were bases and foul lines.

For stoopball, all you needed was either a stoop of stairs or a curb, two guys, and the trusty Spaldeen. The "batter" would throw the Spaldeen against the stoop and the other guy would have to catch it and field it. And, as in every neighborhood, we had our own rules for what counted as a single, a double, a triple, and a homer.

Like stickball and stoopball, punchball was what it sounded like. We would "bat" by punching the ball with our fist. Maybe the most primitive form of baseball ever, this was something only kids could create.

If punchball was about brute force, Hit the Penny was about finesse. The object was to hit the coin with the ball and even better, to make it flip over. A hit brought one point, a flip was worth two. We'd play to eleven or twenty-one or until we got bored. There was also slapball, box baseball, and "A" My Name Is Alice. So you see, a Spaldeen could keep you going for quite a while. But when there wasn't a Spaldeen around there was always Scully. Mumbly-Peg. Stretch. Johnny-on-the-Pony. And, one of my favorites, Ring-a-leavio.

Ring-a-leavio was like Capture the Flag, except there was no flag. We would divide up the neighborhood—half would be the hunters, the other half the hunted. I'd say it was like hide and seek, but hiding for too long was poor form. If you were the hunted it was a lot more fun to "show" yourself and get chased. The chase was everything.

If you got caught, the hunters would yell, "Ring-a-leavio, caught, caught, caught," and escort you to jail. In our neighborhood, "Ring-a-leavio, caught, caught, caught," developed to "Ring-a-leavio, Coca-Cola."

Jail in our neighborhood was often just a designated tree. To free the prisoners we'd try to sneak up as close as we could and then make a run toward the jail—one person would draw out the jailer while the other busted through to free the prisoners and yell, "Home free all." On any given summer night, the sound of kids yelling could be heard on almost every street in the Bronx.

Of course we weren't always outside yelling during Ring-a-leavio; sometimes, we were inside chanting another phrase that summed up my childhood: "Need 'em, need 'em, got 'em, got 'em, need 'em, got 'em, got 'em, need 'em, got 'em, need 'em," the endless litany as we went through a pack of baseball cards.

The whole idea was to create a complete set. So if you didn't have 'em, you needed 'em. And if you got 'em and someone else needed 'em, and someone else got 'em and you need 'em—you traded 'em. But only if you had doubles. And if we weren't trading cards, we'd be flipping or scaling.

To flip, you would take a card by the edges and with a deft swing of your arm, let it drop. The other guy would flip his card and try to match it, face up or face down. If he did, the card was his, if not, it was yours. Scaling was basically taking a baseball card and with a Frisbee-like motion, sending it as far as it could go. Sometimes the guy who threw it farthest would win. Other times we would scale it against the wall like pitching pennies: Whoever got closest to the wall would win the card.

We used all our cards. Mays, Mantle, Snider. We were just kids so we didn't know that there was anything special to having their rookie cards. And as I got older, my mom, thinking I was no longer interested in my cards, threw them away. I could hardly blame her. Not after I lost Willie Mays's autograph. I had a collection that today would be worth thousands of dollars. There was no way she could have known. And I still love her. Losing my Willie Mays autograph was another story.

It began like an ordinary day at the Polo Grounds. The pitchers warming up, the guys stretching on the sidelines. We had seats in the upper level; even from there, my idol, Willie Mays, was larger than life. But we'd always go down to the field level before the game just to get a little closer.

Some of the players were hanging around, tossing the ball. I started yelling, "Willieeeee, Willieeeee. I'm over here." I actually got his attention. He looked at me, then came over. I don't think I said anything, I just stuck out my program and he signed it. Unbelievably, I got Willie Mays's autograph.

Sixteen innings later, I lost it.

It was 8–all, bottom of the sixteenth, when Valmy Thomas, the catcher for the Giants, came to the plate. Thomas parked a home run and the Giants won the game 9–8. In all the excitement, I left the program on my seat. I didn't realize until I got home and then it hit me—"Oh, God, this is the worst thing that ever happened to me." I had Willie Mays's autograph . . . for five hours.

I didn't think I would ever get over that day. But I did. In fact, I had repressed it entirely until just last year when I took my son Jake to Dodger Stadium. He'd been before, but this was his ninth birthday. I was fortunate enough to have arranged ahead of time to bring him on the field during warmups to meet Davey Johnson and the players.

In the weeks before the game, Jake and his friend Jacob Moss had made a little clay sculpture that looked like a four-leaf clover. Jake would go around the house saying, "I made this for Shawn Green. If I ever get to meet him, I'm going to give it to him." I never gave it a second thought. Then there we were standing with Shawn Green and Jake put his hand in his pocket and pulled this thing out. I remember the dialogue perfectly:

Shawn Green: "Well, what is this? Is this a good luck charm?"

Jake: "I don't know. I think so. I hope so."

Shawn: "Tell you what. If I hit a home run today, I'll keep this in my locker."

Jake: "Cool."

If I hadn't been there I wouldn't have believed it but just like in a movie, Shawn Green hit two home runs that day. Jake and his buddy were jumping up and down cheering and going crazy. As I sat there watching Jake, I hoped he would never forget it.

ROB REINER is a director, actor, and children's advocate. In addition to his Emmy-winning work as a star of the long-running hit television series *All in the Family,* Rob has directed many acclaimed films such as *Stand By Me, When Harry Met Sally . . ., A Few Good Men,* and *The American President.* In 1997 Reiner and his wife, Michelle, founded the I Am Your Child Foundation in order to raise public awareness about early childhood development.

## ABOUT THE EDITOR

Steven A. Cohen is a vice president at Ogilvy Public
Relations Worldwide in Washington, D.C. Born in
Baltimore and educated at Washington University in
St. Louis, he joined Bill Clinton on the campaign
trail directly after college and worked as a press aide
to the new president starting in 1993. He rose to become the First Lady's deputy director of communica-
tions before taking his current job. Steven Cohen
lives in Kensington, Maryland, with his wife and
daughter.